Newham

᛭ 03/09		
NW 6/09		
1 1 JUL 2009		
- 4 AUG 2009		
2 0 MAY 2010		
1 9 APR 2011		

24 hour automated telephone renewal line
0115 929 3388
Or online at www.newham.gov.uk

David Carpenter

DOCKLAND APPRENTICE

BEARS

HIDE

Published by
Bears Hide Publishing
2 Bramber Avenue
Peacehaven
Sussex
BN10 8LR

First published 2003

ISBN: 0 9546488 0 3

Printed in Great Britain by Antony Rowe Ltd
Bumper's Farm, Chippenham, Wiltshire SN14 6LH

Dedicated to all apprentices past,
present and future.

Contents

List of Plates

Acknowledgements

I would like to thank the many people who have helped and encouraged me to write and complete Dockland Apprentice, among whom were:

Bob Aspinal	Museum in Docklands
Burnard Copleston	Friend and Critic
Bob Hunt	Antony Rowe Ltd
Dr. R.J.M. Carr	Photographs and assistance
Donald Mackenzie	Photographs
John Radford	B.B.C. Southern Counties Radio
Lucy Pringle	Museum of London
Mary Edwards	National Maritime Museum Greenwich
Mary Mills	Greenwich Borough Council
Philip Neumann	Foto Flite
Pipa Gordon	B.B.C. Southern Counties Radio
Richard Joseph	Publishers
Suzannah Dunn	B.B.C. Southern Counties Radio

Introduction

Dockland apprentice follows many of the experiences of the writer through his five year apprenticeship as a marine engineer in the London Docks during the 1950s. It gives an insight to the social history of the docks during a period that was considered by many, to be the halcyon days of British Merchant Shipping.

He briefly covers his first acquaintance, at an early age with the docks, and how it influenced him to take up a sea going career.

To the general public, the docks were regarded with a certain amount of suspicion, and were thought of as a mysterious and inaccessible area, possibly because they were usually portrayed in films of the period as the centre for organised crime.

He describes how difficult it was to obtain an apprenticeship within the docks, especially if you did not have any family connections. Then goes on to give an insight, as to what life and working conditions were like in the docks and on some of the many ships that he worked on during his apprenticeship.

More importantly he features some of the people that plied their trade amongst the vast complex of the docks, and describes in some detail the more eccentric characters that he worked with.

Also mentioned are the eating places and pubs that were part of the infrastructure surrounding the largest enclosed dock system in the world almost half a century ago.

He briefly covers, the power and influence that the unions had on the different trades within the system, with what were known as restricted practices.

The London Docks and the magnificent ships that used them, together with the thousands of specialised workers that were required to operate them have now drifted into history. Many of the docks were filled in, and through lack of forward planning, much of the architectural history has been lost forever.

Economics and technology did in a remarkably short time, what the might of the German air force, with all their saturation bombing raids on the docks during the second world war failed to accomplish.

D. J. Carpenter 2003

Chapter One

The First Day

It is often said that you should never return to a place after a long absence, should you do so, you would probably be disappointed by what you see. Never was there a more vivid example than the London Docks now known as Docklands.

To all those thousands of people who made a living there up until the 1970s, and have not returned since, the change would be hard to comprehend. Along the stretch of the river Thames from Tower Bridge down to Woolwich was to be found the most concentrated dock system in the world. Encompassing the Pool of London; St. Katherine's Dock; London Docks; Surrey Docks; Millwall and West India Docks; East India Dock; Royal Victoria; Royal Albert; and King George V Docks, known as the Royal Group of docks, plus all the river wharves and cuts.

The docks were a world of their own, even to Londoner's not connected with them and yet living within a stones throw they were a mysterious and forbidding place, mostly hidden behind enormous walls. The people that obtained their living amongst this vast system covered almost every trade known to man, many of a highly skilled and specialised nature.

A common phrase often heard, was when someone was talking to a neighbour about someone living in their street that worked in the docks, who perhaps had recently acquired a motor car or was going away for a holiday was. "Well of course he works in the Docks." This implied that he had some sort of illegal income, which in fact could not have been further from the truth.

It was in 1946 that I made my first visit to the docks, I was seven years old when our next door neighbours took me along to meet their son who was returning from overseas war service. Although it was only a distance of about three miles, it was the furthest that I had ever travelled. This was

11

because of the war, where the need to keep close to the air raid shelter had been paramount, as we were constantly under threat from the German flying bombs, such as the 'V' one, or Doodle Bug as they were called, and in the later stages the deadly 'V' Two Rockets from which there was no protection. We spent most nights in our Anderson Shelter which for some reason was at the bottom of the garden and smelt of damp blankets and Kerosine, it was also inhabited by a large coloney of aggressive black beetles. If the air raid siren went during the day my mother either put me and the dog under the table, or in the cupboard under the stairs next to the gas meter. There was some logic in this, as several houses in our area that were destroyed by flying bombs had their stair cases still standing.

The journey to the docks involved a short bus ride to the Woolwich ferry, where we boarded one of the ferry boats for an exciting trip across the Thames to North Woolwich, always referred to locally as over the water; then another bus whose destination simply said the Docks. It was only a few minutes ride before we were seeing ships so immense, that they towered over the terraced houses that lined southern edge of the Woolwich docks.

This was the Royal Group which comprised of the Royal Victoria, the Royal Albert, and the King George V docks; with a water area totalling 230 acres. Joyous reunions were had, as my neighbours son disembarked from a ship of unbelievable size, and we returned home by another route seeing many more ships on the way. That visit left a lasting impression on me, especially the ships, many of them had names on their sterns that were all new to me, such as Hong Kong, Panama, San Francisco; where were those places, and what were they like. I made up my mind that one day I would go to sea on one of those dark mysterious and purposeful looking leviathans.

As the years passed I made many more visits to the docks. My mates and I would travel back and forth on the Woolwich ferry, which since opening in 1889 has always been free. The reason for this was that as so many people worked on the opposite side of the water to where they lived, all kinds of leaky old vessels were used to get from one side to the other, quite unsuitable for the Thames with its fast tides and rip currents. Consequently many lives were lost, so the government of the day passed an act to provide a free ferry service from North to South Woolwich. There were usually three vessels in operation at the same time, with a fourth on the gridiron, which was sighted just downstream of the North bank terminal. This vessel could always be seen having repairs carried out to its paddle wheels by the ship repair firm of R.H.Green and Silley Weir.

The ferries were called, Squires, Gordon, Will Crooks, and John Benn, they were all built on the Isle of Wight, the first pair in 1922–23, and the second two in 1930. Each paddle was driven by a separate horizontal steam engine, and the boilers were fired by coke from the Beckton gas works just down stream. They were capable of carrying 1000 passengers and 100 tons of vehicles.

The Thames during the 1950s was unbelievably polluted, so much so that if you were unfortunate enough to fall in, it would automatically mean that you had to spend 24 hours in hospital, with all the required injections and associated treatment. However this did not deter us and many more youngsters from taking a dip from a stretch of foreshore on the North side just down stream of the ferry terminal, commonly known as the beach. In fact it was here that I learnt to swim. There were many factories that lined the banks of the river, the most concentrated stretch was probably from Wapping down to Woolwich, where there were to be found, lead works, tanneries, guano works, glue factories, margarine factories, various chemical plants, sugar factories, rope makers, foundries, power stations, gas works, cable makers and many more, all using the river as a convenient dumping medium for their industrial effluent. Upstream of the Isle of Dogs the river banks were mostly lined with warehouses.

When the Woolwich ferry manoeuvred at the boarding jetty, which was reached by a long walkway leading down a floating pontoon, all of which was kept in position so that

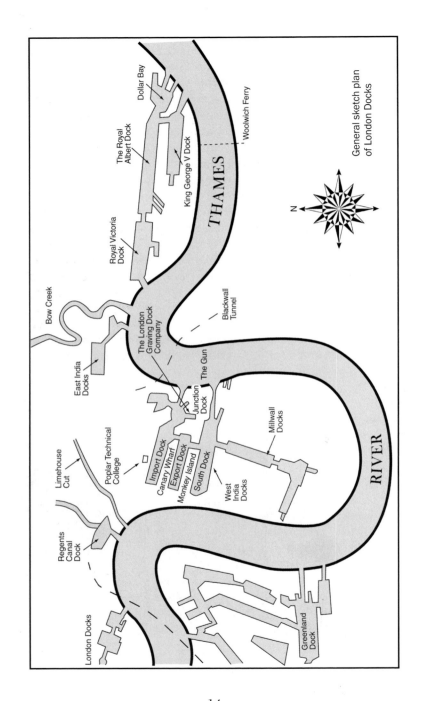

General sketch plan of London Docks

it could rise and fall with the tide by giant wooden piles. The paddle wheels churned the river into a brown froth often reaching several feet in depth, and creating a strong pungent aroma, quite unique to the area around the ferry. On hot summer days the river could be smelt up to five miles away. It was quite common to hear people greet each other with "Good morning, the rivers up today." Referring of course to the nasty smell that pervaded the whole area. I think it must have been the Woolwich ferry that gave me my ambition to become a marine engineer; I used to spend hours watching their engines. Passengers had access to the corridors down each side of the engine room, which had windows on each side, but with no glass in them, so you could stand on the slatted seats which were in fact life rafts, and with elbows resting on the sill of the opening, have a grandstand view of the machinery, which to my young eyes seemed of gigantic proportions. The other factor was the inviting smell of hot oil and steam which wafted out of the engine room. When the telegraph rang the chief engineer would move the handle in confirmation of the manoeuvre required, then move a

A sad farewell to The Woolwich Ferry's 'John Benn' at the end of her days. 1963. (Museum in Docklands).

large lever, and turn a handwheel and the engine would suddenly rev away amid a hiss of steam and a fascinating hollow clonking sound.

One of my favourite places was on deck against the boiler casing, from this vantage point a good view of the river and the passing shipping could be had, and at the same time you were kept nice and warm, especially during winter. My school days were coming to an end, I had applied for an apprenticeship with the main ship repair firms on the river, such as Harland & Wolff, and, R.H. Green & Silley Weir, but without success, the problem being, apprenticeships were not given on academic qualifications alone, preference was given to sons and nephews and so on. I was lucky in as much, that a near neighbour, who happened to be an Admiralty inspector put in a good word for me at the London Graving Dock Company on the Isle of Dogs. This was mainly because I had an old racing Norton International motor bike, which he took great interest in. I used to let him have a burn up round the block on it now and again, and I am sure that without the Norton I would never have had the opportunity to go into the marine engineering business.

London Graving Docks Advertisement from circa 1959.

One morning a letter came from The London Graving Dock Co, instructing me to attend for an interview the following week. I duly presented myself at their offices in Prestons Road, Poplar, on the Isle of Dogs, and was taken up to the works manager's office and introduced to Mr Riley. He was a big man in his mid sixties with a ruddy complexion and was smartly dressed in a dark three piece suit; I also noticed a bowler hat hanging on a large coat stand. He pointed to a chair, indicating me to take a seat in front of a large desk which had blueprint drawings, some wooden patterns together with various mechanical parts scattered about its top, plus the usual items of office equipment. After introducing himself, he asked me why I wanted to be an apprentice engineer with The London Graving Dock Company. Whatever my answer was, he seemed satisfied that I was worth giving an opportunity to. I mentioned that I had not received my G.C.E. results as yet.

"That's of no importance, I will give you a six months trial period, we will soon see if you are any good, if the foreman thinks you have the right abilities, we will sign you up for an indentured apprenticeship, which will be for five years. Report to the timekeeper's office downstairs next Monday morning at 7:45 good luck! Oh, and bring a boiler suit with you."

I returned home feeling very pleased with myself, having been given the chance of a start in the marine industry with one of the top ship repair firms on the Thames, and yet somewhat apprehensive as to how I would find things on my first day.

I arrived at the time keeper's office on the Monday morning, where I was given a brass disc about 35mm in diameter which had the number 1220 stamped on it, and was told that I had to keep it all the time I was employed there. It was to be handed in every time I left the yard, and collected on arrival. It was also explained, that if I arrived one minute after 8am I would lose a quarter of an hour's wages, and if I arrived after 8:15am I would lose one hour's wages, and it was no use giving the excuse that I had caught a bridge (there was a dock entrance each side of the main gates, with a swing bridge on the north side and a cantilever bridge 200 yards to the south), if it looked as though I was going to be late I could always get off the bus, and walk across the lock gates and come the rest of the way on foot. I was then told to wait while they found someone to take me over to the fitting shop. After about five minutes, a young man came down from upstairs and introduced himself as Sid, and then asked me to follow him. As we walked along he explained to me that he was working in the drawing office until he was sixteen, then he would be

Advertisement for AYR Engineering & Construction Co Ltd. Circa 1959. Part of The London Graving Dock Co Ltd.

It is interesting to note that the site of the Orchard Dry Dock dates back to the very beginning of British maritime history. During modifications in 1946 wooden piles were exposed that were identified as being part of a Roman floating wooden cradle.

From the mud was extracted a large flint ball, believed to be the ammunition for a Roman war machine. These machines would have been launched into the river from the wooden cradle.

Many ships were built here for the Navy and the famous East India Company. The Orchard Dock was also the site of the first iron shipyard, and also where the first screw driven ship for the navy was built. This was the Royal Yacht 'Fairy'.

This was also the place where the pioneers who founded the first English colony in America (Virginia) set sail from in 1606.

joining me in fitting shop, we got on well from the start and remained good friends all through our apprenticeships.

Sid escorted me over to the fitting shop, I say over; because it meant crossing over the caisson, (pronounced kasoon) which was the entrance to the dry-dock. We had to go right round the dry-dock, passing the boiler maker's shop on the right, then the electricians and the welders, before coming to a pair of large sliding doors facing the dry-dock itself, this was the entrance to the fitting shop.

As we crossed the caisson, to the right and ahead of us, moored against the quay of Blackwall Basin, lay a Royal Navy

London Graving Docks, Dry Dock looking North towards the Caisson. The building on the right with the tall sliding doors was the Plumbers Shop. The entrance to the yard was between the Plumbers shop and the building with the gabled end, this was the general stores. The upper floors of both buildings were part of the offices.
The top of the entrance lock to Blackwall Basin is just visible to the right of the caisson. (R.J.M. Carr 1979).

destroyer which was being worked on, in the dry-dock itself was a ship called the Liverpool Packet. There was ship's equipment lying everywhere, anchor chains, winches, piles of rope, ventilators, masts, and all manner of seemingly abandoned gear scattered all over the place.

The Fitting Shop, where if all went well, I was to spend the next two years was vast. Down the middle was a roadway wide enough to take the largest of lorries. It was the beginning of July, a bright sunny morning, but on entering through the large wide open doors, the whole place was in semi darkness with sunbeams coming through small windows down the length of the roof, and penetrating a layer of smokey haze about twenty feet up from the floor. At the far end of the shop I could see a pair of doors, similar to the ones we had just come through. I noticed to my right, three large diesel generating sets, one of which was running.

Sid explained that they supplied the whole yard with electricity, and that they were cooled by water which was pumped up to the top of a wooden lattice from where it then cascaded down into a large tank on top of the welder's shop, it then gravitated back down to the generators. He then went on to say, we now had to make our way down to the far end of the shop, where he would hand me over to the foreman. On the way he pointed out the various machine tools, some of which seemed enormous compared to the schoolroom size I was familiar with. There were massive radial drills, huge lathes, plus a very large planeing machine which was opposite the generators.

At the far end of the building, to the right of the doors, were some offices, these were crude affairs, built on the end of the wall out of plywood and corrugated iron sheets. Sid took me into the larger one, where there were several people looking at some blueprint drawings. The door was open, and as we entered Sid gave a knock and they all looked up and one of them walked across to us with a welcoming smile.

"Ah ye must be thee nee apprentice, all keen te make a start the noo I expect." He was in his early sixties, a grey haired, rather stout person, wearing a grey double breasted suit, who introduced himself as Mr Taylor the foreman.

Mr Taylor or Bill Taylor as he was known by everyone, thanked Sid for bringing me over, who then made his way back to the drawing office.

"I'll tak ye roond te the charge hand the noo," said Mr Taylor.

He then led the way next door to the charge hand's office, which resembled an observation post, it was reached by a short flight of wooden steps, and the front had a large window which looked out over the whole workshop. Here I was introduced to George the fitting shop charge hand. George was about five foot, two inches tall of slim build, his dark hair was combed back flat, with a parting in the middle emphasising his widow's peak. He had a rather long nose and a permanent stoop, making his head seem to stick out in front of his body giving him a hawk like appearance. He wore a brown three quarter length overall, a dark blue shirt and a red tie. In fact I never saw him wear anything different all through my apprenticeship, I can only assume he had a collection of blue shirts and red ties. I was to learn later that he was known as 'Niff-Noff,' owing to a speech impediment that combined a sort of lisp with on occasions a stutter which became more pronounced the more annoyed he got, which was quite often as far as apprentices were concerned.

Nevertheless, during my years at the Graving Dock I found him to be a kind and helpful person. Before he was made up to charge hand he had been a highly skilled turner, this was probably where he had acquired his stoop like posture, as round shoulders and poor eyesight are a legacy that lathe operators have to bear. George took me over to the fitter's area, explaining on the way, that it was here, providing I passed my trial period, that I would be spending the next two years, after that I would go outside, this meant being put with a fitter and his mate to work on ships throughout the dock system.

George introduced me to Joe McKie, one of the fitters, then returned to his observation post saying that Joe would show me the ropes. Joe McKie was a person that you could not help but like, we got on well right from the start. George having told Joe my name, suggested that we might have a problem, it transpired that the other apprentice in the fitting shop was also called Dave. Joe said that as the other Dave was bigger than me, he would henceforth be called Big Dave, and I Little Dave, so that any problem of confusion in future was soon solved. I had brought a new blue boiler suit with me which I put on, feeling rather conspicuous amongst all the old hands. It was then that big Dave appeared, apparently he had been on an errand to the yard stores which was near the main gates. Joe introduced us, and said it might be a good idea if Dave gave me a tour around the yard to familiarise me where everything was. Just then a little old white haired man appeared from round the end of the bench carrying the biggest teapot I had ever seen. It was brown enamelled and the handle had been sawn off, and replaced with a piece of oily looking rope.

"This is Little Arthur, one of the shop labourers, he always makes the tea," explained Joe. "Have you got another mug, we've a new apprentice started this morning," he added. Arthur had bought an extra mug, as he had seen me arrive; and before Joe had finished speaking Arthur banged it down on the bench and filled it with steaming hot grey brown liquid which he pronounced as tea! Joe and Dave produced their mugs and Arthur filled them in a continuous pouring motion, which left a large puddle on the bench, he then carried on without saying a word to the other side of the shop to give the turner's their tea.

"He never says much," commented Joe. Whatever it was that Arthur had poured out, went down well, even though every now and then a piece of enamel would ping off; float on the surface for a second or two, but never quite long enough to flick it clear, and then disappear into the depths of the mug. After tea, Dave said that we might as well start with the fitting shop and work our way round the yard in the opposite direction from where I had entered earlier. I was introduced to the other fitters, of which there were four, then we went over to the other side which was the turner's domain. There were nine lathes ranging in size from small six inch toolroom examples to enormous machines up to about 35 feet (10 metres) in length, these were mainly used for machining propeller shafts. There were milling machines, a large boring machine, a circular saw, and two gigantic radial drills, the largest could take a 4 inch drill bit. Alongside it was a large rectangular concrete pit, about 6 feet in depth, in this was a cast iron drilling table onto which large components could be secured for drilling. Then there was the planing machine which Sid had already pointed out as we came in earlier. There were also various small drilling machines and grinders, all the machines were independently driven by their own electric motors, the only exception being the screw-cutting machine which was situated just inside the main doors next to the foreman's office. This fearsome antique was still driven by the remains of the original overhead system of fast and loose pulleys.

To the left hand side of the doors was the engineer's stores, which covered a large area and was enclosed by heavy gauge wire mesh, this was the domain of Fred the store-keeper. It was also the congregating point for the outside fitters and mates while waiting for orders. There was every conceivable tool that could be needed in Fred's stores. Dave explained that if you wanted a tool such as a drillbit, tap or die, or a file, you exchanged it for your brass disc with your number on it, when you returned the tool you got your disc back. Needless to say the apprentices had a good racket going manufacturing brass discs for tools that were lost, or went astray for whatever reason. Fred also had a large bin full of abandoned discs, that he didn't know what to do with. We left the stores, turning right outside the main doors, we followed the quayside round until we came to the Shipright's shop. There was a lot going on inside, two ship's lifeboats were being overhauled, and I noticed a brass bound companionway (ladder) having the finishing touches put to it, plus various wooden cabinets were being made.

There was a strong smell of teak and linseed oil in the air, quite different from the fitters shop, which smelt of a mixture of white water, [cutting oil] and Stag, which was a thick red liquid, that came in a tin with a stags head printed on it, and was used as a jointing compound for just about every type of joint known to the marine industry. When new it had the viscosity of paint, and was used for jointing, as it got older, it thickened up and was used for serious leaks, as time went on, and especially if the lid was left off, it obtained the consistency of putty, and could be used to plug quite big holes. We left the Shipright's and went next door to the Rigger's Loft, here there was an overpowering smell of hemp and tar.

After the Riggers we went on to the Boiler-maker's and plater's shop, this was even bigger than the Engineer's shop, it was difficult for Dave to explain the workings of the place,

The London Graving Docks dry dock looking South. On the left can be seen the Southern end of the Blacksmiths Shop with the chimney cowls of two of the forges visible on the roof. Behind the long concrete wall to the Southeast was Prestons Road. The wooden skin floor of the dry dock can be seen exposed at the far end, with the culvert to the pump room just showing above it. The dry dock could be emptied from full in one hour, making it possible for a ship to be docked, scrubbed, painted and undocked in under seven hours (known as a wash and brush up). The entrance to the fitting shop was situated on the West side just behind the Portacabin. (Photograph circa 1979 R.J.M. Carr).

owing to the deafening noise. There was a constant machine gun sound, only higher pitched, coming from the pneumatic hammers, together with a continual crashing and clanking of heavy metal plates being moved around, sheared, or bent to shape. The air had a red tint caused by the rust from the plates, which when dropped, would send up dense clouds of red dust. The workers wore weird heavy leather outfits evolved from years of experience. Dave pointed out some of the heavy machinery, there was a massive rolling mill, a guillotine, banks of drills, and large presses, which were all being worked. Now and then great showers of sparks from metal cutting equipment would rain down on all and sundry.

We left the Boilermakers with a taste of rust in our mouths, and our boiler suits covered in a layer of fine red dust.

"We'll go over the caisson to the Plumbers, I'll point out the main stores on the way, then along to the Blacksmiths,"

The large plate bending rolls in the Boilermakers and Platers shop that was situated on the West side of the dry dock.
Photographed prior to the auction of stock at the end of The London Graving Docks days in the West India Dock. (R.J.M. Carr).

remarked Dave. The Plumbers was more civilised than Boiler Makers, it had a smell of Linseed oil, putty, and white lead in the air. There were two plumbers and an apprentice in their workshop at the time we arrived. Dave introduced me to them, and they went on to explain that the major part of their work consisted of the repair of sanitary systems, port holes, and windows, at the time of my visit they were in the process of bending up a length of large diameter copper pipe.

We left the Plumbers and then carried on along the side of the dry-dock, which Dave informed me was 450 feet long, 62 feet wide, and 22 feet over the sill, and was built in 1878. We passed a large travelling crane, which could traverse the length of the dry-dock on a pair of railway lines, and then came to a ramshackle arrangement of buildings, on top of which, standing like a clump of toadstools was an array of chimney cowls, this indicated to me that this must be the Blacksmith's. This was confirmed as we walked under an old corrugated iron lean-to roof, the ground was covered with lengths of iron, piles of shackles, anchor chains, old iron troughs, and various heaps of newly forged components.

"Well this is the Blacksmith's," said Dave.

We entered through the remains of what was once a door, and it took a minute or so to make out our surroundings as it was almost dark inside. There were windows in the roof and in one wall, but they were coated in a thick layer of grime, some were broken and it was through these that what light there was came in. There were two forges going, out of the six or so that were spaced around the shop, as my eyes became accustomed to the gloom, I noticed a large pneumatic hammer down at the far end just past a pair of forges. A large area of floor was covered with bending plates, these were about 5 inches thick and had rows of 1inch holes drilled all over them. The main source of light was coming from the forge just inside the entrance, where the Blacksmith was hammering a piece of white hot metal on an adjacent anvil. He was an elderly, thin wiry man, wearing a leather apron which came up over his chest, under this he had on a string vest, the other thing I noticed were his boots, they looked like the type that cowboys wore.

With him was his mate, who was holding the piece of metal being forged in a pair of long tongs. After he put the work piece back in the fire to reheat, Dave introduced me to Albert the Blacksmith, and his mate Harold, who was wearing a suit that at one time had probably been his Sunday best, it was now nicely coated with a metallic sheen that made it impervious to any further dirt or rust. Strangely he also wore a necktie that he had tucked into his waistcoat. We left the Blacksmith's shop, which had been much bigger than I had expected, and continued on round the dry-dock.

A photograph taken by R.J.M. Carr (circa 1979) of part of The London Graving Docks, Blacksmiths Shop, looking North. Prestons Road was behind the wall on the East side. The forge on the left was in constant use during the writers time at the Graving Dock. Due to the photographers skill it is possible to see everything in great detail, but when in operation it was impossible to see more than a few yards in any direction due to the smoke laden interior and the grime covered windows.

"I had better show you the bog's while we're here," said Dave, leading the way to a long narrow corrugated iron lean-to, a few yards along from the end of the Blacksmith's.

"You have to be in a pretty desperate plight to come in here," he said as he showed me the way in. I soon realised what he meant, there were four cubicles, resembling starting traps at a greyhound stadium, opposite the first one, hanging on a large hook was an old telephone directory. At the back end of each cubicle was a plank with a hole in it. The sides of the cubicles were of galvanised steel sheet and to anyone sitting on the plank they would have been about shoulder high. There were no doors, a quick look through the hole in the plank, showed there was a long drop down to what appeared to be the main sewer, Dave then told me, that he thought there must be a manhole somewhere in the Blacksmith's shop, as it was not unknown to have bundles of burning newspaper come drifting down the pipe while some desperate unsuspecting person was on the throne.

"I think it gets flushed through when the dry dock is pumped out through the calvert at the head of the dock into the river," he explained.

"If you like we can go on board the 'Liverpool Packet' and have a look round the engine room before we go back to the shop," he added. The 'Liverpool Packet,' was a steam driven cargo vessel on charter to Bowater's, the paper making concern whose main factory was down river at Northfleet. I didn't know it then, but it was a place I would frequently visit later on in my apprenticeship, to work on Bowater's own ships which were mostly powered by Sulzer diesel engines. One of the things I remember most, was their excellent canteen, coming a close second to Tate & Lyle's superb facility of a non profit making works canteen that we always patronised, when working on the sugar boats at their Silvertown wharf.

The 'Liverpool Packet' was quite an old ship but still in excellent condition, she had to be as she made regular voyages across the North Atlantic between the pulp mills on the East coast of Canada to the U.K. and the Continent. She was powered by a Triple Expansion steam engine, a 'Three

Legger' as they were generally called, and crewed entirely by Canadians which was where she was also registered.

She wasn't a large ship for the task that she had to do, probably weighing around 3000 tons. We had a good look around, keeping a low profile, not wanting to be in the way as the Graving Dock fitters and heavy gang were in the process of removing the low pressure piston. The noise down below was deafening, the platers were busy renewing a section of platework below the water line and the ear piercing noise from their pneumatic hammers made it impossible to talk.

Dave signalled to me, pointing his index finger in the air several times, that it was time to go back on deck. We climbed up the series of ladders and stepped out of the engine room, to a beautiful sunny morning. I could still hear the platers riveting away down in the Dry Dock and as we made our way across the gangway I looked down to see that they were working on a staging about 6 feet below the water line. On the bottom of the dock they had a small furnace going, heating up the rivets, every now and then, at a signal from one of the men on the staging, a red hot rivet would be tossed up to him which he caught in a huge pair of asbestos gloves, it was then picked up by a second man with a pair of tongs and placed in the appropriate hole, a third man then put the riveting gun over it, there was a fourth man inside the ship with another gun, at some unseen signal the rivet was then hammered home. Dave then said that we had better make our way back to the shop as it was nearly time for lunch. We left the ship and continued on round the southern end of the dry-dock, passing the pump room used for pumping it dry, and on towards the fitting shop entrance that I had entered first thing that morning.

"Have a quick look in here, its the chain testing pit," said Dave.

It was a long corrugated iron shed, but only about six feet wide, inside was a long narrow trench and at one end, some hydraulic machinery and a large dial gauge reading in pounds and tons. "This is where all the chains, shackles, and wire strops are tested," explained Dave. We left the chain testing shed, and entered the fitting shop where it took a few seconds to become accustomed to the gloom. As we passed the generators I noticed someone leaning over the guard rail with both arms outstretched over the flywheel of the generator that was running, he was holding a block of wood about 18 inches wide which had emery cloth attached to it, and he was polishing the flywheel which was something like 8 feet in diameter. Dave noticed me looking, and explained that Ernie, who looked after the generators did that twice a day, and it was reckoned that they had lost several inches off their diameter since he took on the job after they were installed in 1947 to combat a fuel crisis. Just passed the generators, Dave pointed out a wide doorway, and said that in there was where the Heavy Gang kept all the lifting gear, and it might be best if we gave it a miss, as they were a rough lot, and considering it was my first day you couldn't tell what they might get up to.

We carried on down to the fitting area passing some very large cylinder heads and liners and various other pieces of heavy ship's machinery, as we approached the bench, Joe looked up. "Had a good look round then, its about time for lunch now, did you bring any sandwiches with you Dave?" he asked. I said I hadn't, so Dave suggested that we could go to the P.L.A. canteen, Kate's cafe, the pie stall just outside the main gates on the other side of the swing bridge or round to the Gun for a drink.

Chapter Two
Aunty Kate's

"Take Dave round and introduce him to Aunty Kate, she does dinners at a special rate for apprentices," said Joe.

"O.K. we'll wash up and go round there then," replied Dave. The washing area was a row of hand basins against the wall just outside the Charge hand's office. A drum of soft soap was provided; soft soap is a creamy brown substance, with a consistency about the same as butter, and a not unpleasant smell. It has many uses in the marine trade, the least effective, being the removal of dirt from hands. Dave explained that if you got particularly dirty there was a drum of Plus Gas (i.e. penetrating oil), over by the stores that would get the worst off. Having washed up, we removed our boiler suits, and Dave led the way out of the fitting shop, round the back of the yard and along the side of a small basin dock known as Junction Dock.

"There's no need to clock off at lunch time," he remarked as we crossed a wood yard where large stacks of Greenheart were stored by The Port of London Authority, (P.L.A.). On our way towards the entrance lock of The West India Dock, Dave told me that work was started on the building of this dock in 1800 and it was opened in 1802, it became known as The Import Dock, the system was expanded with the construction of The Export Dock, which opened in 1806. It was the first totally enclosed dock system in London, with very high walls and its own security force. The water area of these two docks was 49 acres, with the basins at Limehouse and Blackwall plus Junction Dock it made a total of 58 acres.

The designer and engineer in charge was William Jessop, the son of Josias Jessop, who was the resident engineer of the Eddystone lighthouse from 1734 until he died in 1761. The excavation and building of the system was a monumental undertaking, using mainly picks and shovels to shift the clay by hundreds of Navvies into horse drawn carts. There must have been an army of Stone Masons required to construct the two and a half miles of usable quayage available, then there was the building of the vast warehouse's and enormous walls that enclosed the complex. It took only two years from laying the first stone, (under which was placed a bottle, within it an inscription in Latin to British Commerce), to the opening day. It was the engineering triumph of its time, and it is doubtful if the time taken to build it could be equalled today, even with all the latest machinery and technical know-how. In 1829 the city canal was incorporated into the system, and became known as The South West India Dock, some forty years later it was linked with the Import and Export Dock, making a total water area of 92 acres, and just over 4 miles of quays. The importance of The West India Docks was borne out, in that they were the first public buildings to be illuminated by electricity, they were followed by Billingsgate Market, Holborn Viaduct, and a section of the Thames Embankment.

We crossed over the lock gates, and Dave led the way towards some railings which were the boundary to the dock. On the other side of these stood a short terrace of Victorian houses, he pointed out that the one next to the railings was Kate's Cafe. As we walked between the railings and some bushes, Dave suddenly stopped, looked around and then removed a section of the railings just wide enough to squeeze through, they had been cut so that the join was invisible to a casual glance. We stepped through the gap and as he replaced the secret section he said, "Best to make sure no one's looking when you come this way."

We were now in an alleyway right alongside Kate's, as we walked down the alley we passed a large sash window that was open, Dave placed his hands on the stone sill and leant forward as far as he could, he seemed to make a point of looking right in. I noticed that it was the kitchen and standing by a large concrete sink was an old woman, who must have been the inspiration for Giles cartoon character of Granny, she looked up and gave us a friendly wave.

"I've got a new customer for you," Dave shouted in.

"I'll tell Kate, she'll look after him," squeaked Granny. We then continued round to the front and entered through the main door. From the outside the place looked old and grimy, just as all buildings did in the area, mainly due to the London smog's, but greatly added to by the smoke from the funnels of ships using the locks alongside. In the case of steam driven vessels it would often be thick black smoke with an oily smell that sometimes tumbled down from the top of the Woodbine like funnels to engulf the whole area.

With the Motor ships, great lumps of carbon, the size of golf balls frequently rained down on all and sundry, as they started their main engines to leave the locks. This was especially so with inward bound ships after a long voyage. As we opened the door and stepped inside, we were hit by a thick wall of tobacco smoke, as far as I could see, there were no empty tables, the place was full of unscrupulous looking characters wearing a motley selection of W.D. clothing, such as reefer jackets, duffle coats, and combat jackets, etc. The interior was long and narrow with a row of tables down each side, each was divided from the next by a shoulder high partition of dark stained wood. I noticed that the tables had marble tops and were spotlessly clean. Most of the tobacco smoke was coming from one particular booth, where one of the occupants was puffing away on a very large pipe, thick clouds were drifting across into the gangway between the two rows of tables.

The occupants of that particular booth were dressed in a sort of naval uniform, that I recognised as that of the P.L.A. Lock keepers. Several of the other tables were commandeered for serious looking card schools being played among an array of steaming hot mugs of tea and ashtrays full of smouldering cigarette ends. It seemed as though we wouldn't get a seat, however through the thick haze, a woman appeared, she looked to be in her late thirties. "Come on you lot, move over, I've got two hungry lads here that need feeding," this was obviously Kate herself.

There was an immediate response, with a general shuffle about and a space was soon made for us in one of the cubicles, this unfortunately turned out to be the one next to the pipe smoker. Dave introduced me to Kate, who was wearing a spotless apron that had some sort of floral pattern and was the type that pulled over the head and was then tied round the back of the waist, on her head she was wearing a red cloth, wrapped round and tied at the front in a large knot.

"Today we've got Irish stew, steak and kidney pie or babies head," said Kate. Not knowing what babies head was, I said that I would have the Irish stew, I later learned that it was a small steak and kidney pudding about the size of a large orange. Kate then went back towards the counter, and quickly returned with two steaming hot mugs of tea for us while we waited for our dinners to arrive. As we were drinking our tea Dave leaned across the table, and with his hand over his mouth, whispered.

"When it comes to the puddings, don't have the apple pie."

"Is it no good then?" I asked.

"No its really good, probably the best you'll ever taste, but today Sinbad, that's Granny's cat is sleeping on top of it out in the kitchen. That's why I always look to see where the cat is when we come past the window, sometimes he sleeps on the meat pie and sometimes on the apple pie, Granny always puts the apple pie by the back window, looking up the dock, and the meat pie by the side window that we passed on the way in, so unless you want to get a hair ball in your guts, choose the bread and butter pudding which she keeps in the oven."

Dave told me all this in confidence, then told me to watch anyone who had the apple pie. After we finished our dinners, we had another mug of tea, and I eagerly watched as Kate served two huge wedges of apple pie and custard to a pair of Lightermen sitting opposite. I didn't have long to wait, Dave kicked my leg, and nodded in their direction where one of them was already extracting a piece of cats fur from between his teeth. The strange thing was that nobody complained or even mentioned it, they gave the impression that it was all quite normal as they hurriedly emptied their plates and pushed them to one side to clear the way for another card school. When it came to pay, Kate said that I only had to pay a shilling instead of one and ninepence, and if I didn't have enough I could leave it until I got my first wage packet. No wonder she was known by the apprentices as Aunty Kate.

We left Kate's and made our way back over the locks towards the yard. There was plenty of shipping in the West India Dock, the vessels lined the south quay into the distance, two main wharf's protruded into the dock from the far end, Dave explained that the nearest one was known as Monkey Island, and the one to the right was called Canary Wharf. He then went on to point out the various shipping company's that used the dock on a regular basis. From where we were standing, it was possible to see ships belonging to Ellermans, Harrisons, Ben Line, Palm Line, and Prince Line, Dave also pointed out a Maru boat from Japan, and a Baron Boat, belonging to Hogarth's, known as 'Hungry Hogarths', they were tramp ships that would go any where there was a cargo to be had. Just coming into the locks from the river, was a ship called Suecia, she was a magnificent looking vessel, more like a large Victorian steam yacht than a cargo ship.

Dave explained that she was one of Swedish Lloyd's regular visitors, and together with her sister ship, Britannia, ran a fortnightly service between Gothenburg and Millwall Dock,

Swedish Lloyd's 4631 tons gross 'Suecia' (1929). Together with her sister 'Britannia', she ran a regular passenger service between Gothenburg and Tilbury. Seen here after leaving Tilbury, steaming up river to discharge her cargo in the Millwall Dock.

which she was now heading for. He went on to say that she was built in 1929, and was mainly a passenger vessel, and what was more interesting was the fact that she carried a complement of Swedish Stewardess's. Unfortunately the Graving Dock didn't carry out repairs to the Swedish Lloyd ships, so we wouldn't be getting the opportunity to work on them! Which was shame.

The whole water area of 151 acres, in total, including Millwall Dock, was a 'potpourri' of craft. There were river tugs, waiting to assist the Suecia on her transit into Millwall Dock, and several small diesel powered harbour tugs, so low in the water, that it lapped over their transoms, that were going about their business rounding up the barges, (known as lighters) that didn't seem to have anyone on board, the tugs gave the impression of mother ducks with their brood. There was a general business like noise emanating from the whole area.

The quick sharp sound of the tug whistles, as they signalled to each other, together with the continual rattle of steam winches coming from nearby ships as they swung their derricks outboard discharging goods from all parts of the world into the waiting lighters. There was the sound of escaping steam from the safety valves high up on the ships funnels, and as the 'Suecia' settled herself in the lock there was the frantic sound of whistles, as the lock keepers controlled the movement of the mooring lines between the ship and the quay.

In the distance, from beyond the North Quay came the clatter of railway goods wagons as they were being shunted about in the sidings which covered the area between The North Quay and Poplar High Street. This is now the site of the new Billingsgate Fish Market. Suddenly all the background noise was obscured by the tooth crunching grinding sound of the gears on the twin bascule road bridge, as it was being lowered after the 'Suecia' had entered the locks.

Then there were the smells! these were as varied as were the sounds, many drifting out of the ships holds as they discharged all manner of commodities. Some were quite scented others such as hides or fish meal were so bad that you tried not to breathe, and ended up having to gulp in vast quantities of foul smelling air to compensate. Depending on the wind direction there was always the heavy aroma of Molasses, mainly from the North Quay, this would be mixed with the sweet smell of recently sawn timber stacked in the large open sided sheds between the Export Dock and Junction Dock.

Over all these intermittent and varied smells, was the soot laden haze from the funnels of the tugs and shipping that relied on their boilers to maintain their power supply. The whole scene gave an impression of great activity, and a sense of adventure especially to the likes of Dave and myself, whose intention on completion of our apprenticeships was to join the Merchant Navy and go to sea. When we eventually arrived back at the yard and entered the fitting shop, Joe was at his bench, he never went out for lunch!

"Right I suppose we had better find you some work to do," he remarked as we approached him.

"We've got all these valves to overhaul, and when we've finished this lot there's another pile down by Niff Noffs office to get on with," he added as he pointed to a large heap of assorted valves, that even to my inexperienced eyes, had broken or missing handles, bent spindles, broken studs, and bent flanges. He went on to explain that there were two main types, steam and water, the big gate valves were for water, and the globe shaped ones were for steam, there were others for fuel oil and some odd looking ones, that he would explain when we got to them.

He then went through the general procedure for overhauling them, saying that we had to strip them down, drill out any broken studs, check the valve seats and if they were too bad to re-cut and grind in, they would have to have new seats machined up by the turners. The old seats would be bored out, and the new ones fitted by us, any new spindles would be made by the turners and the square ends to take the handles would be given to the apprentices to file to shape.

They then had to be cleaned and reassembled and the glands repacked with steam or greasy packing, depending on the type of valve.

"These little ones with the long cone shaped seats are called cocks! they are to be found mostly on the boiler face, we have to lap in the plug, that's the cone shaped piece and then pack the grooves down the sides, we call this stemming, with a mixture of asbestos and graphite flakes," explained Joe.

"Which reminds me, we are out of asbestos, go round and ask Slim if he has any," he added.

The benches were divided by a partition along the back so that it was not possible to see or talk to the fitters around the other side without actually going round there. The other side was the domain of Slim, who was also the shop steward, and Mike Seaton, an ex-sea going engineer. At right angles to them, a few yards up the shop, was another bench, this was the home of Jimmy Goodbody. Jim kept himself to himself for most of the time, he was a short quiet spoken person, with a balding head, and an easy sort of manner, always willing to help and give advice if asked for. I went round and asked Slim if he had any asbestos, he had a look round, under the bench and in the cupboards.

"No we seem to be out of it, you'll have to go down and see George the charge hand, get an order then go over the main stores and get a tube, make sure its blue!," he replied, as he still continued to look. It all began to seem a bit funny, and it looked as though they were setting me up, as I knew they did to new apprentices.

As I didn't have any choice, I went down to George's office and explained that we needed a tube of blue asbestos.

"If you take this over to the general stores by the offices, Harry the storeman will sort it out for you," said George as he wrote out an order and handed it to me.

I went back and told Joe that I was going over the stores.

"O.K. don't get lost, and watch your step," he replied.

It was definitely looking suspiciously like a set up of some sort, I thought to myself as I made my way round the dry-dock towards the stores. I went in through the small door, which was marked Stores, there was a long counter covered in thick linoleum behind which were rows of shelves reaching up to the eaves of the roof, they were all full of consumable items some of which I recognised, such as coils of gland packing, tins of jointing compound, large rolls of jointing material, rolls of caulking cotton, boxes of screws, and lots of metal bins of nuts and bolts. At one end there were coils of rope, various sorts of lifting tackle with more bins of shackles and eye bolts. There appeared seemingly from nowhere, a little old man wearing a brown overall and a greasy cloth cap, known as a cheese cutter, he had on a pair of horn rimmed spectacles which sat on the end of his nose, so as he looked at me, with his chin touching the top button of his shirt, it was across the top of his glasses. This must be Harry I thought to myself, I handed him the order and explained who I was.

He took the ticket without saying a word and went off to the far end of the stores, rummaged about under the counter and came back with a tubular cardboard carton about 4 inches in diameter and 18 inches long under his arm. He set it down on the counter, saying "One tube of blue rinse," and disappeared back into his secret hiding place without another word. The manner of his behaviour, with quick and jerky movements, and the way he came out of his sanctuary, reminded me of a pet hamster. What did he mean by blue rinse? I was to discover this in due course. Well at least it wasn't a set up as I thought it might be. I returned to the fitting shop having completed my first task, and gave the tube to Joe.

"Right here's what we have to do," he said as he opened the end of the carton and pulled out a handful of the blue asbestos, and then started pulling it apart until it became a fluffy pile on the bench. Taking a handful of graphite flakes, he mixed it into the pile of asbestos, by the time he had finished it was everywhere, the sunbeam which came through one of the windows in the roof now beamed itself right across the bench, lighting up a whole mass of glistening particles as they drifted over the surrounding area. Joe had already stripped and lapped in one of the boiler cocks, so he proceeded to show me how to pack the plug with the asbestos and graphite mixture using specially made stemming tools, made from lengths of copper about 6 inches long and a quarter of an inch wide. By tea break at 3pm, we had finished four cocks, both Joe and I were covered in blue fluff, it was in our hair, up our noses, and all down the front of our boiler suits, no wonder Harry called it blue rinse! by modern day standards, there was enough asbestos drifting about to have a small town evacuated.

Little Arthur came round with his enormous tea pot, he was known as Little Arthur because one of the other shop labourers, also named Arthur, who could have doubled for Jack Palance the well known film star, except Arthur was twice his size, was known as Big Arthur. Big Arthur drove the overhead crane, it spanned the full width of the shop and could traverse it's complete length. It was used for all the lifting jobs in the shop, such as lowering tailshafts into the big lathe, placing large jobs under the radial drills, onto the planer and boring machine. It was in almost continuous use throughout the day, and made a terrible noise as it made its way up and down the workshop.

It progressed with a grinding rumble with intermittent high pitched screeches as one of the locomotive type wheels slipped on the overhead rails, due to a flat on one of the rims. It was something that could have easily been fixed, especially as the shop had more than enough equipment and expertise, it was a typical case of the cobbler and his shoes. How long it had been like it I never knew, but it was still the same five years later when I left The Graving Dock to go to sea. The strange thing was, there was a complete spare crane wrapped in sacking parked at one end of the shop that I never saw move.

Big Arthur was a quiet person, and I always treated him with the greatest respect, I was told that during the war he had been one of the Desert Rats in North Africa. When I left the fitting shop after two years to go outside, coincidentally Big Arthur also left and joined the outside Heavy Gang, so that I regularly worked in his company. He liked to play tricks on the ships native crews, most of whom were very superstitious, and I remember one time, we all had to evacuate the ship because of one of his pranks. He would often greet you with a slap on the back, and if you were not ready for it, your teeth would jar to the point of breaking. He was certainly a man to have on your side!

The whole heavy gang were a law unto themselves, they were all very big people, except for Archie their foreman. He was about 5 foot seven inches in height, quite slim and wiry, but what he lost in size he made up for in toughness, I heard him referred to as, tough as a bag of old nails.

We would have our tea in a small area between the end of the bench and the wall of the shop, it was partitioned off with a bulkhead onto which was built a bench type seat. On the end of this furthest from the wall was another bulkhead slightly wider than the seat, facing the seat and protruding into the shop, some ten feet away was another bulkhead the same width as the seat, this was where we hung our coats. Under the coats and in the corner was a pile of coke, used for fuelling the large cast iron stove, which looked a bit like a Darlek from the T.V. series Dr Who. This was sited in the middle of the area between the two bench seats, the outer wall, and the main bench. There were several of these stoves situated around the workshop, they stood about six feet high and were around two feet square, and had a door near the base which flapped down for shovelling in the coke, this faced out towards the shop. They were massively constructed and had slots going through them, like letter boxes to give a more effective heating area. With the onset of winter a fresh delivery of coke would be added to the existing pile, which made it difficult to hang our coats.

Little Arthur was in charge of flashing up the fires, keeping them banked up and cleaning out the grates every morning, so that once they were lit, they never went out until the weather improved in the spring. The letterbox sections were ideal during really bad winters for warming up tools and at tea breaks for toasting sandwiches. This operation required a certain amount of skill, when Little Arthur wasn't looking we would put in two or three shovels of coke so that the lower part of the stove would be glowing red hot. A sandwich put in the letter box, and not retrieved almost instantly would result in it being reduced to a burnt offering. These little areas where we had tea, and sometimes played cards were known as holes in the wall, there were quite a few around the perimeter of the workshop. There was one further up the shop, behind a row of cylinder liners, that actually went right through the wall, into a kind of bunker built under a vast pile of Greenheart logs in the timber yard outside, from where it was completely invisible except when a card school was in progress. During these times cigarette smoke could be seen drifting out from between the logs.

This particular hole in the wall was destroyed a couple of years later, when a P.L.A. employee happened to spot the smoke and thinking the timber was on fire called the fire brigade. The card school were completely unaware of the developments going on outside, until tons of water came cascading through the logs quickly filling the whole area to the point where it actually came through the hole in the wall, and flooded a considerable expanse of the fitting shop floor. The card players rushed out dripping wet hoping to blend themselves in with the general goings on in the shop before they were spotted by any of the management, if this had been the case it would have meant instant dismissal. As it was there was hell to pay, the general manager, Edgar Taylor who had succeeded Mr Riley was not a very nice person at the best of times, went to great lengths to find out who the culprits were; luckily without success. He also had the hole in the wall bricked up, and a thorough search carried out for any further such places.

He then started making surprise visits to the fitting shop, picking on anyone seen standing about and wanting to know exactly what they were doing. For some reason he made a point of singling out the apprentices and giving the unfortunate victim a hard time, with threats of instant sacking and tearing up their indentures. This would all be done at the top of his voice, with much arm waving and his face going quite purple until the blood vessels in his temples bulged to bursting point.

A good early warning system was developed from both ends of the workshop, so that we could all be at our benches or machines when he stormed down the shop. You then had to keep your head down and hope that you were not the one that he picked on. Knowing that he always wanted an exact breakdown of the job that you were doing, and should there not be an official job in hand at the time, we all had our standby jobs ready just in case. Mine was a set of bearing scrapers that I always kept handy just in case I was the unfortunate victim, as was often the case! Strangely he never queried the length of time I was taking to complete them, in fact I never did finish the complete set.

Chapter Three

The Tunnel

My first day at the Graving Dock was coming to an end, when about 3:30 Niff-Noff came round to see if anyone wanted to work overtime. Joe explained to me that all overtime rates were paid at double time, so it was always worth doing. Depending on the job in hand, it would be 7pm, 9pm, or 11pm, sometimes an all nighter, although apprentices were not allowed to work all night. Up until 7pm was known as a Half Turn, 9pm was a Turn, and 11pm a Turn and a Half.

This particular night there was a Half Turn going, which meant an extra four hours pay, i.e. half a day which was about four shillings and eight pence, or 23p in today's money. I decided to put my name down and give it a go. Niff-Noff came round and said I would be working with Reg Manser, giving him a hand on the boring machine. Reg did all the boring work and also operated the big lathe, which machined up the propeller and tail shafts, etc.

The boring machine was only a few yards down the shop towards the stores, although I had seen Reg working the boring machine, I hadn't been introduced to him, so I had no idea what he was like. Niff-Noff took me across and introduced us, he was the perfect Friar Tuck from Robin Hood, he looked exactly like the character portrayed in the movies of that name. He wore a brown knee length overall that he kept done up down the front, this was quite an achievement because his stomach protruded out in front of him to the extent that he wasn't able to see his feet when looking down.

I got on well with Reg, he was only too pleased to show me how the boring machine worked and how to operate such a heavy piece of machinery. The job that had to be done that evening was to machine out a valve seat in a large pump casing to receive a new one that was being machined up by Eric on one of the big lathes across the other side of the shop. Even though they were working to blueprint drawings, it still required a lot of going back and forth between the boring machine and the lathe on the other side of the shop. That was where I came in, it was my job to pass on any dimensional changes from one to the other. Reg was a very quietly spoken person and I had some difficulty hearing what he said above the noise of the machines and the general background sounds from around the shop. At 5:30 Little Arthur came round with the tea, so while we were knocked off for ten minutes I was able to ask Reg one or two questions.

Instead of reading his paper he willingly went over what we had done and explained what we were going to do next. His attitude was typical of all the fitters and turners, including labourers who I knew during my five years at the London Graving Dock. One of Reg's characteristics was his snuff, he would produce a small tin from the top pocket of his overall every ten minutes or so, then place a pinch of it on the back of his hand and give it a good sniff, shutting his eyes as he did so, this was invariably followed by a panic like grab for the nearest piece of rag to have an uncontrollable sneezing fit into. The front of his shirt and overall were always covered with it, and were tinged a yellow brown colour. He also kept a large reserve tin in an old wooden box that was fixed to the wall, which he referred to as his locker, for topping up purposes.

We managed to complete the job by 6:45 so Reg said we might as well get washed up, the two hours seemed to have flown by, and what was more I was going to get paid for four hours. I rejoined Dave who had been overhauling valves, and we made our way up the shop to the main doors by the dry-dock, this was where all the fitting shop workers and the heavy gang gathered to wait for the whistle that announced it was clocking off time. We didn't actually clock off, but handed in our brass discs at the main entrance, the timekeepers had two methods of collecting the discs. One was to bring out two, sometimes three long boxes, similar to a money box, they had four brassbound slots in the top, they then hung them on brackets fixed to the opposite wall to the time keepers office, into these we had to drop our discs, the other was to open the sash window in the office and the discs would be put through on to the desk inside.

Well that was the theory of it! What actually happened was that when the whistle blew there was a mad rush across the caisson by all the yard workers, mostly on foot, some on push bikes, mopeds or motorcycles, and the odd car. Anyone who thought they had been hard done by on their time keeping by the timekeepers, took this opportunity to have their revenge. It was a race to get to the timekeepers as they hung up the boxes before they could gain sanctuary back in the office. If they were not quick enough they would often be swallowed up in the crowd and be suitably dealt with, often emerging after the crowd had passed very dishevelled and quite often with a nice dollop of black grease on their heads or in one of their pockets. Some evenings when they knew there was going to be a high percentage of angry workers who had lost an hours money, this usually occurred when there had been a bridge that morning, they would open the sash window of the office instead of hanging out the boxes. This resulted in everyone throwing their discs through the window as hard as they could, to the extent that the timekeepers had to take cover below the desk. The wall behind showed the battle scars of what thousands of brass discs had done over the years. There would then be a rush for the gates, the bigger the mass of workers the better, as there was less likelihood of being pulled up by the P.L.A. dock police and being searched, a good example of the safety in numbers syndrome found with animals in the wild.

The problem with being stopped and searched was that it could delay your departure for half an hour or more, once out of the dock, it was only a few yards to the bus stop and a few minutes wait for a bus, followed by a ride half way round the Isle of Dogs to the foot tunnel under the Thames to Greenwich, then another bus to Woolwich and home. A total journey time of about an hour and a quarter, this was providing I didn't catch a bridge at the West India Dock entrance, as this would mean at least another half hours wait. So if I was unlucky enough to be pulled by the police and then get a bridge, it would make me at least an hour late in arriving home. Consequently it was impossible to make definite arrangements for my evenings and as we worked Saturday mornings, i.e. a forty four hour week, it meant Saturday afternoons were the same.

I mentioned this to Joe who suggested I come in on my motorbike, he had a Ariel Red Hunter and side car which he used every day, it was a fairly new machine, where as mine was a twenty five year old Norton International thoroughbred racing bike, not at all suitable for heavy rush hour traffic. I decided to give it a go, but I was a bit apprehensive, as it meant going through the notorious Blackwall Tunnel, which in those days was still a single tunnel with two way traffic.

Every morning the queue would go right back up Tunnel Avenue to the British Oxygen depot, some two to three miles from the entrance to the tunnel. With the bike I could go right down the outside of the queue until reaching the tunnel approach, this was about four hundred yards long and still bore the scars of enemy aircraft shells from the war, the tunnel together with the whole of the dock system was a prime target during the conflict.

The writer on his 1933 'Norton International'.
Note the bicycle lamps and frame modifications. (Circa 1956).

47

There was a narrow walkway about 15 inches wide with a very high kerb that went through the tunnel, if it was possible to get up on to it, a much quicker if precarious transit could be made through to Poplar. To be held up in the tunnel due to a breakdown, or two lorries meeting on one of the bends, where neither one would reverse, creating an hour long stalemate was an absolute nightmare experience. The exhaust fumes were so dense that it was only possible to see as far as two vehicles ahead, the problem was made even worse because no one ever switched off their engines for fear that they would not be able to restart them once the hold up had sorted itself out. The police very rarely entered the tunnel, so in the main it was left to the drivers themselves to sort out any problems.

Once I had overcome my initial worry, I used the bike quite regularly, even in the depths of winter, and despite being quite unsuitable it proved to be very reliable. I did have a bit of trouble with it one morning when it overheated and seized up just before I got to the ventilator shaft on the Poplar side of the tunnel. I had no option but to leave it at the bottom of the shaft and take to the stairs which brought me out near the riverside about 100 yards from the Graving Dock. I actually clocked in early, much to the surprise of the timekeepers.

When Dave arrived we sneaked out through one of the holes in the wall and went back down the tunnel. The intention was to see if we could manage to get the bike up the stairway and push it round to the yard. Luckily by the time we got back to the machine it had cooled down enough to free up the engine. We decided to see if it would start, so while Dave held up the traffic I ran with the bike and gave it a bump start. To our relief it roared into life, Dave climbed on the back, there was no actual pillion seat! he had to make do the best he could. I took it easy, and managed to clear the tunnel and get back to the yard through the main entrance to the West India Dock.

Parking the bike in the wood-yard we casually entered the fitting shop hoping that we were not spotted by Niff-Noff the charge-hand. Although we had been out for over an hour, no one seemed to have missed us, I told Joe what had happened and he replied that he thought something was wrong as he had seen the Norton parked at the bottom of the ventilator shaft as he came through on his Ariel.

It always took Joe much longer to get through the tunnel than myself, because with his sidecar he had to stay in the traffic queue, where as I was able to go down the outside whenever the opportunity presented itself. I didn't fancy riding the bike home that night, so at lunchtime I bought it into the fitting shop and parked it inside one of the several spare cylinder liners that were stored there. I soon had the engine stripped down, where I found only a slight scoring on the piston, this was soon rectified and I was able to box it up the following day.

The weeks went by very quickly, Sid had now joined us in the fitting shop from the drawing office, and we also had another lad join us, who went by the name of 'Speedy'.

Aerial view of The West India Docks 1950's looking towards London.
The London Graving Dock with a ship in the dry dock and another moored alongside in Blackwall Basin can be seen just to the right of centre, between the two dock entrances.
The long building with the white roof adjacent to the dry dock was the fitting and machining shop during the writers apprenticeship. This view makes an interesting compaison with the 1802 image by William Daniell. (Museum in Docklands).

He was always getting into trouble for being cheeky, this was a big mistake! Especially where the heavy gang were concerned, they certainly gave him a hard time for the short period that he was with us. Unfortunately after about three months, he slipped while messing about, and fell into the drilling pit of the large radial drill, badly injuring his back. He was taken away in an ambulance and that was the last we saw him.

Big Dave had now left us to work outside, his two years in the shop being up, he would spend the next three years with a fitter and his mate working on ships throughout the whole dock system. It was customary that if you got on o.k. with the fitter that you had been assigned to, then you would stay with him for the rest of your apprenticeship. My six month trial period had long since passed, and as nothing had been said to the contrary I assumed that I was accepted as an indentured apprentice.

Just before my trial period was up, I was put on the screwing machine, this contraption was considered the worst machine in the whole shop. It was very old, certainly of the Victorian era and it required a great deal of patience to master it, as

William Daniell's aquatint of The West India Docks in 1802 looking West towards London. Blackwall Basin is in the foreground. The house's on the river front are in coldharbour. (Museum in Docklands).

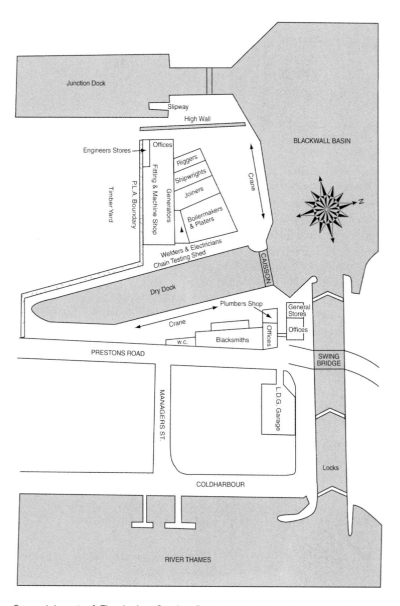

Junction Dock

Slipway

High Wall

BLACKWALL BASIN

Engineers Stores

Offices

Riggers

Shipwrights

Joiners

Boilermakers & Platers

Crane

Fitting & Machine Shop

Generators

P.L.A. Boundary

Timber Yard

Welders & Electricians
Chain Testing Shed

Z

CAISSON

Dry Dock

Plumbers Shop

General Stores

Offices

Crane

w.c.

Blacksmiths

Offices

PRESTONS ROAD

SWING BRIDGE

MANAGERS ST.

L.D.G. Garage

Locks

COLDHARBOUR

RIVER THAMES

General layout of The Lodon Graving Dock during the writers apprenticeship.
1956–1961

continual adjustments had to be made to make it perform accurately. The other unpleasant thing about it was that it was situated just inside the main doors opposite the stores and adjacent to the foreman's office. In the Winter months it was a very cold area, the main doors were never closed during the day and the machine was out of range of the coke stoves further up the shop. When operating this infernal contraption your hands would be continually sprayed with cutting fluid and after a very short time your boiler suit would become saturated all down the front and up the arms. It looked like milk and was known as white water, it also had a very strong smell, not unpleasant as far as I was concerned, but my mother used to say that I reeked of it when I arrived home. No matter how much I washed myself the smell would continue to leach out of my skin, making it rather embarrassing when going out for the evening. The other thing was that your hands and especially the fingers would wrinkle up as they do when immersed in water for any length of time. This made them very soft and susceptible to cuts which were very frequent indeed, as the edges of the threads and swarf (waste metal) were extremely sharp. The cuts took a long time to heal, probably due to the cutting oil, so that at the end of the day my hands would be in a pretty bad way, any plasters put on in the morning would be washed away by tea-break.

The job that I was given, was to cut and thread all the tie rods for the building of the new Tilbury Jetty. It was not possible to wear gloves owing to the continual fine adjustments that had to be made. It took me three weeks, every morning Niff-Noff would give me a list of what sizes were required, and how many, they ranged from 2 to 6 feet in length, and 1 to 2 inches in diameter, with varying lengths of thread on each end. The first two hours were always hard going, after that the machine began to warm up, even the white water warmed up and not so many adjustments had to be made to maintain accuracy. Eventually Niff-Noff gave me a sheet of paper for the days work and said.

"You will like this lot today Dave, its the final batch, I bet you're pleased about that!"

I think that the time spent on the screwing machine might have been the final test to see how I coped, faced with a long hard job. Some years later when I went to sea, most of my voyages began from the Royal Albert Dock at Woolwich, and as we passed the Tilbury Jetty on our way down river I would always be reminded of the hours spent on that infernal machine.

One morning while working on a valve chest, I cut the inside of my thumb quite badly, Niff-Noff told me not to bother with the first aid department, which was only a corner of the general stores where Harry the store-keeper plied his second job as first aid officer. His reputation was somewhat dubious regarding treatment, it had been known for him to use a staple gun to stitch up bad cuts.

"Go along to Poplar hospital, take Side with you, you'll get seen to properly there," he said. Poplar hospital was situated at the end of East India Dock Road opposite the entrance to the Blackwall Tunnel, so it only took us about ten minutes to walk there. It didn't take long to stitch up my thumb, they were obviously used to shipyard workers coming in with all sorts of injuries covered with rust, soot grease, marking blue, and smelling of fuel oil, and usually with a coating of asbestos on top of everything.

On the way out Sid suggested that we stop off for a cup of tea in one of the many cafes in the East India Dock Road. During the 1950s the premises in this road consisted mainly of bespoke tailors, ex W.D. surplus clothing shops, and cafes.

If you happened to stop to look in the window of one of the many tailors, almost by magic, someone would appear beside you with a tape measure around his neck, and start to measure you up for a suit. We were dedicated followers of fashion in those days, so we had a good relationship with all the tailors in the area. Phil Segal was the most popular, and together with his son Stan made the finest suits in East London.

We decided to go into Farina's cafe, just outside Blackwall Tunnel. This establishment was run by Mario and Alberto who were twins, together with their mother, who as the name suggests were Italian. The twins worked on serving the customers, while 'Mumma' worked somewhere upstairs in the kitchen, at the other end of the dumb waiter, as far as I know she had never been seen.

The dumb waiter was an ingenious contraption, it was a continuous loop of trays that could be operated from up or downstairs electrically by a button. The dirty plates were put on the up going trays and meals came on the down going trays, the whole apparatus was concealed in the wall, except for two cupboard like openings, one for up, and one for down. The orders were shouted into the up going shaft by one or other of the twins in their very pronounced Italian accents.

"Two spaghettis, anda onea styke anda onyons Mumma," this was the only indication that 'Mumma' was part of the business.

The tea's and coffee were made by the twins at the counter with a tea machine which dispensed twelve mugs in one go. The mugs were placed in a special tray, that located them in two concentric dish like impressions in its base, the tea on the inner circle and the coffee on the outer one. They were filled via an arrangement of tubes, fed from two main tubes, one connected to a coffee machine and the other to a tea machine. This was a great asset to a busy cafe like Farina's.

Mammas bolognese was considered to be the best money could buy, so the place was always crowded. I often had a meal there, before going to night school at Poplar Technical College on a Wednesday evening. I usually had steak and spaghetti, the steak was always horse meat and I suspect that the bolognese was made from the same. Horse meat was readily available in the docks, it was quite common to see horse carcasses stacked up in the West India Dock, they were easily identified by the green looking meat, which I think was caused by the dye that was used to show they were not fit for human consumption, they also had thick layers of yellow fat running through them. Horse's were fast disappearing from the streets of London, their loyal services to the milk, bread, and brewery deliveries were being dispensed with in favour of the diesel van or lorry.

I never noticed any green tint to Farina's steaks, perhaps it was lost in the cooking, it didn't really matter where the meat came from, as it was devoured with great gusto by all of Farina's customers. Perhaps more to the point, I never heard of anybody becoming ill. As usual the place was very busy, Sid and I entered through the grime covered front door, which was largely due to its proximity to the tunnel entrance, we stepped into the tobacco smoke filled interior to find that all the tables were occupied.

Chapter Four

The Duke

"Its pretty full, it looks as if we will have to sit with the Duke," said Sid as he rubbed his eyes and pointed to a table that only had one occupant and three empty chairs, it soon became obvious to me why no one else was sitting there. The individual that Sid had described as the Duke was just about the dirtiest looking person that I had ever set eyes on. He resembled a tramp, except they usually made some effort to keep clean, where as the individual before me couldn't have washed in weeks. He had three or four weeks of stubble on his face and his long grey matted hair, branched out like a leafless bush from beneath a battered and sweat stained Trilby hat.

He was wearing an old grey 'Mackintosh' that was stained all down the front, and as it was not done up I could see that he had on a Fair-Isle pullover which was even more stained than the raincoat, to the extent that it was impossible to distinguish the colours. Strangely he was wearing a Merchant Navy tie, with a very crisp knot, the effect of this was lost by his grubby shirt collar which curled up one side more than the other. As we sat down I was tempted to look under the table to see what he had on his feet, but he looked up and I thought better of it.

"Hello Sidney old chap, how the devil are you, awfully good of you to drop by."

I was quite surprised by his accent, it was certainly not from the East End, more like an Oxford graduate. Sid went up to the counter for the tea's, leaving me with the Duke.

"Just started in the business then old boy? He asked.

I replied that I had been with The Graving Dock for just over six months as an apprentice engineer.

"Excellent," he replied. "You have to make sure you read the best books on the subject, make sure you get a copy of this one."

As he spoke he pulled an old piece of paper together with

a fountain pen from the inside pocket of his raincoat, wrote down the title and slid it across the table using the palm of his hand as if it was a secret message. I took it from him, and as I looked at it I was completely taken back. The name of the book that he recommended; *Questions & Answers on the Marine Diesel Engine, by John Lamb*, had been written in perfect copper plate, the best hand writing I had ever seen. I then realised that The Duke was not the average down and out that I had taken him for. Sid then came over with three mugs of tea and gave one to The Duke, who made a great show of acceptance.

"Not working then?" asked Sid.

"Unfortunately not at present Sid, I am currently on the stones," he replied.

The stones being the terminology used to say that you were out of work, but on the labour pool waiting for a ship to arrive that required repairs. The various ship repair firms on the river would then draw any extra men they required from the pool, as and when needed. We drank our tea's, while The Duke gave us well meaning advice, and decided that it was time to get back to the yard. On the way back I asked Sid if he knew how The Duke had got his name. Sid then related to me how it had come about.

At the time, The Duke was working for The London Graving Dock Co. as an outside fitter, apparently he was in a much worse state than when we had just seen him. The charge hand on the ship, told him that he was an absolute disgrace to The Graving Dock, and unless he smartened himself up he would have no alternative but to lay him off.

The next morning with perfect timing, just as most of the workforce were making their way aboard, a chauffeur driven Rolls Royce limousine pulled up alongside the gangway. The chauffeur, went round the rear of the vehicle and opened the nearside passenger door, out stepped an immaculately dressed person wearing a top hat and tails, complete with a white silk scarf. He made his way up the gangway, followed by the chauffeur carrying a small suitcase.

From that moment he became known as 'The Duke'.

They made their way down to the engine room, followed by

an entourage of fitters and mates. After opening the suitcase on the engine room desk, the chauffeur then produced a brilliant white boiler suit together with a pair of white gloves, which The Duke put on after removing his evening suit. The chauffeur put this on a hanger, also produced from the suitcase, and hung the outfit up in the engine room stores before departing the ship. Apparently no one made any remarks, probably because they were all too stunned by what they had just witnessed. The Duke went about his work, and at 5pm the limousine returned, the chauffeur went down into the engine room and helped The Duke change out of his still white boiler suit, which he had gone to great lengths to keep clean, and then left the ship. The limousine then slipped silently down the quay, amid great cheers and waving from the ship, towards the dock gates, where it was waved through in a manner befitting royalty.

The next morning, The Duke having made his point, went on board in his usual dirty clothes as though the day before had never happened, the difference being that he was now known as 'The Duke'. Sid went on to say that before The Duke came to work in the ship repair yards he had been a senior chief engineer with The Cunard Shipping Co.

Unfortunately he had developed a drinking problem which led to the sorry state that he had been reduced to, brought about no doubt by the horrific war time experiences that he must have been through on the North Atlantic convoys where he must have looked through the gates of hell on many occasions.

We arrived back at the yard in time for lunch, and decided to go to the P.L.A. canteen which was only a short distance away. The food there was passable, the trouble being that what ever you ordered tasted much the same, the tea and coffee were identical in flavour, the only difference being the colour and the price. The main attraction of the place was in the large amount of tables that were accommodated in the dining area, this allowed the card schools to proceed without fear of being requisitioned by the odd few workers that actually wanted to eat there. The card schools were taken very seriously, Solo and Three Card Brag being the most popular. After lunch we strolled back alongside junction Dock to the yard.

As I was slightly incapacitated with the cut on my left hand, Niff-Noff put me with Joe on the Planeing Machine, right up the other end of the shop, this was relatively clean work machining the bedplate of a steam generator. The days flew by and my hand soon healed up, so I was put back overhauling valve chests, white metalling and fitting bearings, and doing machining jobs on the various lathes.

I had been in the fitting shop for just over eighteen months when the union called all the tradesmen out on strike. The only people allowed to enter the yard were the staff, i.e. foremen, managers, and office workers, and of course the apprentices who in theory were not allowed to strike, as it would contravene their indentures.

There had been talk of a strike for some time, Slim, who was one of the shop fitters was also the shop steward, explained to me that no one was in favour of a strike, but they had to comply with the union directive on a national vote to come out on strike for more money. Such was the power of the unions!

Slim was always good to the apprentices, making sure that they were not disadvantaged in any way. He was very tall, well over six feet and always wore a well washed blue boiler suit that never seemed to get dirty. Like many marine engineers he walked with his head bent forward, a habit developed from years of working in ships engine rooms, ducking under low pipe work, crossbeams, and protruding valve handles. He also had an additional habit of using the insides of his arms to hoist up his trousers beneath his boiler suit, he would usually do this as he came up to talk to someone.

The first morning of the strike was like a holiday as far as the apprentices were concerned. There was no one to give us any jobs to do, Bill Taylor the foreman was in, but he was over in the main offices meeting with the managers. This seemed like a good time to strip down and overhaul the old Norton.

Bill Taylor seeing that Sid, Big Dave, and myself were seemingly busy never bothered us for the next few days. On the Thursday however, the formidable Edgar Taylor made an unexpected appearance in the fitting shop, the early warning system not being in operation due to the strike, he caught us red handed. We were all on the lathes, I was machining some new bearings for the Norton, Big Dave and Sid were deeply engrossed manufacturing pokers for which there was a big demand, this was because every household had coal fires in the 1950s.

I think he was more surprised than us, as I am sure he had completely forgotten about the apprentices, what with all the problems the strike must have caused the management. He was on his way down to Bill Taylor's office when he suddenly realised that the lathes were being worked, the only other person in the fitting shop was Ernie, polishing the flywheel on one of his beloved generators.

The first thing that we knew about Edgar's presence was when he shouted at the top of his voice, with the blood vessels at the side of his forehead about to burst. "What the bloody hell's going on here."

There was no point in trying to make up stories as to why we were using the lathes, the evidence was all before us, a box of unfinished pokers lay beside one of the lathes, plus an assortment of motor-cycle parts were scattered about the bench top. He came over and put his foot under the box of pokers, and with some effort, turned the contents out across the floor, shouting.

"Get this junk into the scrap bin."

He then added as he stormed off down the shop, shouting that he would soon find us something useful to do. Soon afterwards Bill Taylor came along and told us to clear a space around a pair of steam driven generators that had lain in the shop for some years, they had been taken off a ship that had been fitted with modern diesel units. They were covered with old sacking that had a thick coating of dust and grime, when we removed it, they looked to be complete except for some external pipes that were missing.

"This lot should keep you all busy for a wee while," said Bill, "Edgar Taylor wants them stripped down and overhauled, you'll have te run up some new bottom end bearings and make new piston rings. When they are finished he wants te see them running on compressed air, if you need any advice come and see me, away the noo."

We thought that we had got off lightly, and set to with enthusiasm but not before we had stashed the pokers in a good hiding place, prior to getting them out of the yard.

The days passed into weeks, with no sign of the strike ending, work on the generators progressed steadily, they had been stripped cleaned and painted.

We had cast up and machined a new set of bearings and had got as far as machining new piston rings, when one morning Bill Taylor came and inspected our endeavours and said it might be a good idea if we had a go at something different for a while.

"There's an old steel lifeboat roond by the shipwrights that could do with some work, after tea go and have a wee look, tell the shipwright apprentices that you are requisitioning it on behalf of the engineering department, then drag it roond here the noo with the Scrutton [electric truck] and some rollers," he added.

Chapter Five

The Boat

It all sounded too good to be true, we hurriedly drank our tea, which we had been making ourselves since the strike began and went round to have a look at the boat. There were in fact, three life boats outside the shipwrights, two wooden clinker built ones, and the steel one, which was much larger than the others. The shipwright apprentices were working on the wooden ones. All three had been condemned by the Ministry of Transport and should have been scrapped, but The Graving Dock usually restored the better ones and donated them to the Sea Scouts. The steel boat was too large and heavy for the Sea Scouts, it also needed some serious platework repairs to the hull, in fact it was a bit too far gone to warrant any repairs at all, but as it was summer time it would give us a good excuse to do some work outside, and make the most of the sunshine. No doubt this had been in Bill Taylor's mind when he told us to leave the generators for a while.

We discussed the possibility of getting the boat usable, and fitting a mast and sails which we knew was obtainable from the shipwrights at a price which would have to be negotiated. It became obvious that we would have to enroll the help of the boiler makers apprentices for some of the platework repairs, which meant they would have to be given use of the boat if we managed to get it launched.

"We'll need a crew anyway," said Sid.

"Let's see if we can find the Scrutton (electric truck) and start to get the boat round near the shop, the best place would be behind the wall, next to the slipway, it will be easy to launch it from there," remarked Dave.

We found the truck in the electrician's workshop where it had been taken to have its batteries charged up, it was a type very common in the docks, with a flat bed, and a control platform at the front where the operator stood and steered it by a lever with an up and down motion. The speed was controlled by a small tram handle which operated in a circular direction. The truck was generally known as 'The Scrutton' after its designer Claud Scrutton. We thought that the batteries might need charging up, but found them to be O.K.

We soon got the knack of handling it, and proceeded to take it round to the shipwrights, stopping on the way to load it with pit props from beside the dry-dock, these were used for keeping the ships upright while in the dock, and looked as if they would be ideal for rolling the lifeboat along on. By the end of the day we had managed to get the boat round to the top of the slipway, which was only just wide enough to accommodate it. The good thing about keeping it here was that there was a wall, some twelve feet high, between the boat and the entrance to the fitting shop, so that it was unlikely that Edgar Taylor would discover our activities.

Over the next few days we cleaned out the inside and got things ready for the boiler maker's apprentices to make a start on cutting and bending the steel plate-work prior to welding it over the worst parts of the hull. It would have been better to have riveted it all in place, but as this would have been a very noisy operation we decided against it, as we didn't want to attract too much attention.

During the rainy days we continued our work on the generators, and when the coast was clear, the poker production proceeded in earnest as this was proving to be quite a lucrative project.

The other diversion was the fact that we had to attend Poplar Technical College for one day and one evening a week. As Dave, Sid, and myself were in different years to each other, we all went on different days, this effectively only gave us two and a half days when all three of us were able to combine our efforts on the poker project. It did however, always enable us to have an excuse, when questioned by Edgar Taylor as to our whereabouts.

Going to college was not top of our favourite activities, but it was all part of the system, and paid for by The Graving Dock so we made the best of it. The evening class, which was always engineering drawing, was from 7pm to 9:30pm, this meant that an evening meal had to be had, sometimes in the college canteen or in one of the many Chinese restaurants just down the road in China Town. This would usually be followed the next day by a session of what is now known as Deli-Belly and would mean frequent visits to the dreaded loo's adjacent to the blacksmith's shop.

The one thing that I always looked forward to after night-school was the ride home on the old Norton. The college had a sort of car park at the side, which was in effect an old bomb site, I used to leave the machine there while at college, it says something of the times in that during the five years that I attended Poplar Tech. I never had any vehicle interfered with while left on the bomb site.

By the end of the evening class, at about 9:45pm the roads were almost empty, I would remove the baffles from the megaphone silencer on the bike, I had made them so that they came out with a twist, a bit like taking out a light bulb from its socket, and put them inside my motorcycle jacket. I would then have to turn on the petrol and oil, back the machine up onto compression, push her down the slope, jump on and let in the clutch, the engine would roar into life with that wonderful sound only possible from an overhead camshaft Norton.

I then had to take it easy, due to the cobbled surface, down Poplar High Street, turning left into Cotton Street and up into East India Dock Road, keeping an eye out for the odd speed cop on his Triumph, then swinging round behind Poplar Hospital into the Blackwall tunnel approach. Then flat out in 2nd gear down into the tunnel taking the first bend at 60mph then into 3rd gear at 70mph down the straight reaching 90mph, not enough road to get into 4th, slow down for the bend then flat out, up and out of the tunnel at 95mph, shutting off at the archway just in case the police were waiting. If I spotted them, I would pull over and refit the baffles with the excuse that they had fallen out in the tunnel.

The whole bike was a bit of a grey area as far as the law was concerned, it was in the days before the M.O.T. and the only lights it had were lamps from a push bike, no good at all in unlit areas. I would arrive home hardly meeting any other traffic, my right leg from the knee down soaking in Castrol R. which always blew out of the cambox. At motorcycle enthusiasts meeting places, such as Johnson's Cafe near Brands Hatch the Manx and International Norton owners could always be identified by their oily right leg and boot.

The strike continued without any signs of an agreement, I never came across anyone that was in favour of it. The union, namely the Amalgamated Engineering Union [A.E.U.] was so powerful that its members had no choice in the matter, they either did what they were told, or lose the right to work in the docks.

Repairwork on our lifeboat was completed to the point where we could launch it down the slipway. With a joint effort of apprentices from the fitters, boilermakers, plumbers, and shipwrights we got her into the water. A quick check to see if there were any leaks, luckily there were not any, and we all piled in for a row around Junction Dock.

It was all a bit of a fiasco in a way, we had four oars, all of them different lengths and sizes, however we did get some sort of system that managed to get us to the other end of the dock and back without anyone falling overboard. After our successful return it was agreed that the next thing would be to get a mast stepped, so that we could rig a sail and take her out of Junction Dock into The Import Dock, this would give us a good reach up to the Western end.

The life-boat project now involved around fifteen apprentices from all trades in The Graving Dock, even the outside engineering apprentices, of which there were four, had become involved. This enabled us to reinstate the look out system for Edgar Taylor.

With everyone contributing, all we needed was a sunny day with a good bit of wind. The following week, the conditions being just right we all assembled at the slipway and made ready. As Poplar College was shut for the holiday period, we had a full complement of fifteen.

The mast was stepped and the sail hoisted and set, it was all a bit chaotic but we eventually cast off, and with gathering speed headed for the cut which took us into Blackwall Basin. We did a couple of circuits of the basin and headed for the bridge across the entrance to the Import Dock, this entrance was flanked on each side by very high open sided timber storage sheds, which was to our advantage as we lost the wind, enabling us to drop the mast and sail to get under the bridge. All went well considering our lack of experience, although there were fifteen of us, there was still plenty of room in the boat as it had been designed to carry fifty people. Once clear of the bridge, we soon had the mast and sail up and began making good headway towards Canary Wharf and the Western end of the Import Dock.

The whole dock was full of ships, which made the area between the quays seem quite narrow for us to turn around in. We had a lot of trouble getting the boat to come about, and ended up alongside an old paddle steamer called the Triton which was laid up at the end of the quay, I was told that she was used as a sea school, and a neighbour of mine recently said that he sat for his Able Seaman's ticket on board her in the early fifties. After a lot of pushing with the oars, we managed to manoeuvre ourselves round to catch the wind and head in the general direction of Blackwall Basin. It took a considerable time to reach the bridge, where we lowered the mast to row under it, as it was now lunch time it was decided to keep on rowing across the Basin into Junction Dock and round to our mooring on the slipway. It was generally agreed that the voyage had been too much like hard work, and was not likely to be repeated and in future we would restrict our boating activities to the confines of Junction Dock, where we could drift about without too much effort. It was perhaps a good thing that we felt like this, because a couple of days later we were summoned to the Dock Superintendents Office. For some reason it was only the engineering apprentices who were called. His office was right next door to the Graving Dock, just the other side of the swing bridge next to Poplar Dock, this dock had the distinction of being owned by British Railways and not the P.L.A. Unfortunately the swing bridge has long since been removed, probably for the road widening scheme, as it was on a tight bend and caused a serious bottleneck for traffic along Prestons Road. However there is still one of the original pillars standing, marking where the main entrance to the Graving Dock was.

On the other side of the swing bridge which spanned the original entrance to the West India Docks, was a pie stall, known as Harriet Lanes, we sometimes went there for our lunch to partake of the delicious meat pies that were sold there. If the weather was nice we would take them out on the pierhead and eat them while watching the passing shipping out on the river. The pie stall acquired its name, after a woman of that name who fell into the machinery at a Chicago meat works.

Opposite the main entrance to the Graving Dock was the beginning of Coldharbour, which still exists in much the same way as it was in the 1950s. This is a very narrow cobbled lane that runs along the river-side and comes out again by the new entrance to the West India Docks. The river side of Coldharbour was lined with some very old properties, such as Isle House the dockmaster's residence, with its bow window to enable the dockmaster to get the first sighting of the East Indiamen as they rounded Blackwall Point. Then came Nelson House, followed by a row of cottages and further on was the River Police's Poplar Jetty where they kept their launches.

Then came The Gun, one of the least known but in my opinion the best waterfront pub on the tidal stretch of the Thames. Fortunately Coldharbour has so far missed the eye of the developers, and remains much the same as it was during the 1950s, its still possible to sit out on the terrace of The Gun and watch the river traffic going by, sadly the great ships have long since disappeared. The Gun was our local pub, and it was almost classed as a criminal offence not to be there at lunch time on a Xmas Eve, after which you would be lucky indeed to make it home before Xmas Morning. Part of the land enclosed by Prestons Road and Coldharbour was used for the Graving Docks transport department, the rest comprised mainly of derelict buildings and old industrial yards. There was also a cafe on the Prestons Road side where we often had a cup of tea and listened to the jukebox. A very high wall marked the boundary of the Graving Dock to Prestons Road, when a large ship was in the dry dock the bow would protrude over the wall, so much so in fact, that when sitting upstairs on a bus it would seem as if the bus was going to collide with the ship. In the early days of the Graving Dock when large sailing vessels used the dry-dock their bowsprits would have protruded right across the road. Sailing vessels continued to use the dry dock right up to the beginning of the second world war. These were mainly in the ownership of Gustaf Erikson of Mariehamn, Finland. They included well known vessels such as the Barque's 'Grace Harwar' and 'Hertzogin Cecilie,' made famous by their grain races from Australia.

We had no idea why we were being summoned to the Dock Superintendent's office, we had been warned by the P.L.A. police on the gate that he was not in a very good mood, and that we were really in for it this time. They seemed to take great pleasure while telling us this as we passed them on our way round to his offices. We were kept waiting for some time, before finally being ushered in before him, he was quite tall, with greying hair probably in his fifties.

"Right," he said, "Let me have all your names."

He then went on to say that it was a serious offence to be in charge of a vessel without an engine in the confines of the dock, this excluded lighters and the like which were in the care of qualified Watermen. Anyone who had read the bye-laws would have known this, so that now we were in big trouble and he wanted to know what we had got to say for ourselves. It transpired that he had been watching us through his telescope, which he had mounted on a tripod by his window from where he commanded an excellent view of most of The West India Docks, in much the same way as the Dockmaster had done from his house in Coldharbour a hundred and fifty years previously. He gave us a serious telling off, saying that if he ever saw us afloat again in the docks he would have no alternative but to report us to Edgar Taylor, where we would get no quarter, and might even lead to having our indentures confiscated. We left his office, thinking that we had got off lightly, especially as Edgar had not got wind of anything.

At last after ten weeks the strike came to an end, and everyone returned to work, a small increase in basic pay having been agreed but it would take years to make up the money lost while out on strike.

I began to take notice of such things, and started to form my own opinions about the trade unions. They were certainly a good thing in the early days of the industrial revolution, where different trades were coming into being and at the same time were being exploited by unscrupulous employers, especially where apprentices were concerned. But it now seemed to me that they had now overstepped the mark, to a point where they had too much power over employers and workers alike. It took two to three weeks for things to get back to some normality, the problem being that as no one knew when the strike was definitely coming to an end, all urgent repairs were being diverted to the continent, which suited the ship owners because of the lack of the

Currie Lines 1955 Zealand (2030) tons gross.
She was the first ship to use the dry dock of The London Graving Dock after the ten week shipyard workers strike in 1957.
Coincedently the first ship to use the dry dock in 1878 was Curries 350 foot 'Edinburgh Castle'. (Duncan Mackenzie).

restrictive practices which were stringently enforced by the unions in this country.

It was four weeks before we had a ship into the dry dock, this was the Zealand one of Curries fleet of short sea traders of 2030 tons. She was a fairly new ship and came in for a check up to her stern gear and a wash and brush up to her hull. There were also some pipe work with attendant valves that kept the apprentices occupied for a while.

After the dry dock was pumped dry so that work on the 'Zealand' could begin, the 'Scrutton' that had mysteriously disappeared during the strike was found upside down at the bottom of the dock. All the apprentices were questioned about the incident, no action was taken but it was generally thought that the boiler makers apprentices were responsible.

After work on the 'Zealand' was completed, her place was taken by a very old Russian coal burning tramp called the Riazan. Sid and I went aboard to have a look around and although old, she appeared to be in good condition, the engine room was nice and clean and obviously well looked after. Contrary to what we had been led to believe, and considering that it was the height of the cold war, we found the crew to be a friendly enough crowd and they were only too pleased to show us over the ship.

As things were still a bit quiet, the outside fitters and mates would hang around the stores waiting for orders, those that were not sent out on jobs would make their way into the fitting shop with the general idea of keeping a low profile. This meant that we would always get a few hanging about our coke fire which we now had flashed up, due to the onset of winter. They would use our hole in the wall for their card schools and generally be in the way, it got to a point where we quite often had no where to sit at tea breaks. We decided that something had to be done about it, one in particular, would stand right in front of the fire with his behind almost touching the fire grate door, to the point where the oil and grease on his boiler suit would begin to melt. Boiler suits were not often washed, to the extent that if one was thrown into a corner, it would probably stand up on its own. We came up with an idea that we thought might put a stop to their hanging around. The plan was to put a bottle of paraffin into the fire with the cork facing outwards and see what happened. We had to wait until lunch time when most people were out, round at the P.L.A. canteen or Aunty Kate's. We found a small medicine bottle in the stores, filled it with paraffin and Sid manoeuvred it with the shovel onto the top of the red hot coke and shut the fire door, we then retired to a safe distance to see what would happen. It took what seemed a considerable time, before there was a heavy muffled explosion and the fire door burst open, followed by a tongue of flame which shot out some thirty feet across the shop and disappeared as quickly as it came.

"That should do the job," said Sid, recovering from his surprise.

"The time delay will give us time to be in the stores when it blows," he added.

He had a point, it wouldn't be advisable to be anywhere near when it blew, as we would automatically be under suspicion for anything like that happening.

The next morning having acquired a new medicine bottle, we kept an eye on the stores, watching for the usual gang to make their way into the workshop. As they came up the shop, we slipped the bottle of paraffin into the fire, shut the grate door and quickly went round the other side of the bench, out of their vision. As they strolled over to the fire, Sid and I crossed over behind the lathes and casually entered the stores. We were talking to Fred the storekeeper, but at the same time trying to keep an eye on events up by the fire, it seemed to take ages. All of a sudden we heard a dull thud, looking out through the wire mesh of Fred's stores we saw a gigantic tongue of orange flame engulf two of the labourers that had been standing in front of the grate. They instantly dived to one side as the fireball shot across the shop and disappeared as quickly as it came, just like the practice one had done.

"Bloody hell," shouted Fred," there must have been a detonator in the coke, I've seen that happen before!"

Everyone made their way towards the incident to see what

had happened. The two labourers were nicely scorched, but quite unhurt, their heavily grease encrusted overalls making them impervious to the quick burst of flame. We thought that we had better join in the crowd, who were all discussing what could have caused it, from what we heard there was no suspicion that the apprentices were involved but we did hear someone else say that detonators and ammunition were often found in the coke, so it was generally agreed that was the cause of it.

However I did spot Jimmy Goodbody whose bench was some yards up the shop, displaying a knowing grin. It occurred to me that he had probably witnessed our trial run the day before, as he usually had his lunch in an alcove at the end of his bench.

The next day we had the whole area to ourselves, so the exercise had proved a complete success, the two scorched victims had walked past our bench and disappeared into the heavy gang's lair.

At times, like we had after the strike, with not much work to do, the regular fitters and mates would be sent on board the Royal Navy Frigate, which was in a moth-balled condition to work. I seem to remember she was called Solarium, but that may have been her class. No one liked working on her owing to the fact that as she was in for an indefinite period, it could be months if not years before they received their P.B.R. (percentage bonus rate), and as there was never any overtime on her they only took home their basic rate of pay, which despite the recent strike was still quite poor.

This was what was known as a hospital job, the other hospital job was in a scrapyard in Bow, where the installation of a hydraulic crusher seemed to go on forever. The Solarium was in the yard when I started my apprenticeship, and it was finally finished during my last year. Some of the workforce had accumulated hundreds of hours on their bonus sheets, so that when it did eventually pay off, they had more money than they had ever dreamed of.

One lunch time, as the sun was out Sid and I thought that we might go for a row round Junction Dock in the old lifeboat. It had lain abandoned on the slipway all through the winter and now looked in a sorry state, everyone had lost interest in it since our run in with The Dock Superintendent. As Junction Dock couldn't be seen through his telescope, we thought we would chance it. After collecting a couple of meat pies from Harriet Lanes we strolled round to the slipway, the intention was to eat our lunch while drifting about on board and make the most of the sunshine. On our arrival at the slipway we were shocked to find the boat with a good foot of water in her, and all the floorboards floating about, I gave her a push with my foot and she slowly moved away from the quay, at least she was still afloat.

"I'll jump in and pump her out," said Sid.

Just as I was telling him that I didn't think it was worth it, he jumped down onto one of the thwarts which broke in two with a loud crack, sending him down into the bilges, where both his feet went straight through the bottom of the boat, taking a large area of the hull with him. It was a good thing that there was only a few inches of water under the boat, otherwise he could have been seriously injured, as it was he landed with both feet on the concrete slipway below.

The water started pouring into the boat, Sid had to sit in it, to be able to get his feet free, once clear he clambered up on to the quay. We made an instant decision to push the boat out over the edge of the slip, where there was a sheer drop of about 25 feet to the bottom of the dock, we had to move quickly as the water was spurting up through the hole and filling her up fast. With some effort we managed to get her to the edge of the slip just as the hull was beginning to settle. It was touch and go for a few minutes as to whether she went over the edge or not, suddenly she tipped up a bit and slid down out of sight into the depths of the dock.

Chapter Six

The Burner

That afternoon, Niff-Noff asked us if we wanted to work half a turn, this was handy because Sid was still trying to get his clothes dry from lunch time and didn't fancy going home on the bus soaking wet. He lived down at Dagenham, near the Ford motor plant, on the way the bus stopped outside the Piccalilli Pickle factory where it was boarded by dozens of Piccalilli girls, who immediately filled the bus with an over powering smell of Piccalilli Pickle. It was a bus ride of terror for any young man unfortunate to find himself on the same bus, and it was often Sid's lot to find himself in this situation, the consequences of being on the bus with wet trousers didn't bear thinking about.

Niff-Noff explained that we would be assisting Big Reg on the large lathe, there was a tail shaft coming in from the Shell Tanker in the dry-dock, which had to be machined down to take a new bearing. It was being craned out onto a lorry and would be with us in about twenty minutes. We worked with Reg to get the lathe ready, so that when it arrived it could be craned off the lorry, straight into position in the lathe by Big Arthur with the overhead crane.

The lorry soon appeared at the doors down at the end of the workshop and came down the centre track, stopping alongside the lathe.

Big Arthur then showed us where he wanted the slings to be put around the tailshaft. We followed his instructions and attached the end of the slings to the crane hook, then unlashed the shaft from the bed of the lorry, gave Arthur the signal that it was all clear and up went the shaft ready to be swung over into the lathe. Sid took one end and I the other, so as to steady it while Arthur lowered it into position. Reg clamped the coupling end to the face-plate, while I pushed up the tailstock so that it was secured in the lathe, we were then able to remove the slings so that Arthur could take the crane down to the other end of the shop to lift some cylinder heads off another lorry that had just come in.

Reg explained that he now had to adjust the coupling end on the face plate, so that it ran true along its length. After showing us how it was done, he started the lathe and took a light cut, after a few minor adjustments it was all ready for the actual machining. As it was now 5:30 and Little Arthur had made the tea, Reg told us to go over and have a break, saying it would take some time to complete the first cut.

As we sat and drank our tea, we could hear the lathe rumbling away as the cutting tool made its slow progress along the shaft. Suddenly there was an enormous bang, followed by a sound like a machine gun being fired.

Before we realised what was happening, the main electricity junction box high up on the wall above our heads exploded with a great flash of flame and smoke, raining down a mass of debris on us. At the same time all the lights went out and the machines ground to a stop. It was pitch black in the workshop, so we decided to stay put and drink our tea, which now contained all sorts of rubbish that had fallen down from the burnt out junction box above us. After a short time we saw a light come on down by the stores, Niff-Noff had found a paraffin hurricane lamp and was making his way, casting weird shadows on the walls of the shop, towards the big lathe. Sid and I decided to join him to see what had happened, and on inspection we found that one of the large gear wheels which was about three feet in diameter had sheared a number of teeth, it had been these that had flown across the shop and hit the junction box. Niff-Noff said there was nothing we could do until the following day, the electricians would have to see to it, so we might as well all go home. A few more lamps, the type used for emergency lighting on ships had been found in the stores, so we were able to wash up and set off home.

The next day we helped Joe repair the gear-wheel, we drilled and tapped it and screwed in steel pegs, it was then taken round to the welders, who built it up with weld. It came back about an hour later, so Joe set up the shaping machine and then re-cut the teeth. By 2pm it was back on the lathe, the junction box had been replaced, so the machining on the tailshaft was able to proceed. While Reg was machining the shaft, Sid and I were put back on to overhauling valves, during the afternoon I had to go over to the main stores to pick up some greasy packing for the valves that we were working on. It was a nice sunny afternoon, so I was able to have a good look at the tanker on my way round the dry-dock towards the stores. I was about halfway along the ship's side, when I heard a peculiar muffled explosion and the whole ship seemed to shake for a second or two. Suddenly a great ball of orange flame followed by a cloud of black smoke shot skywards from one of the inspection hatches on the deck. There was some shouting and people running about the deck, then I heard someone say, "Blimey George was down there."

After a minute or two a pair of gloved hands, then a head and shoulders appeared out of the circular hatch, it reminded me of a mole looking out the top of his mole hill.

"What the bloody hell happened there," I heard the figure shout.

This was George Lilly, one of the most eccentric characters in the Graving Dock. He emerged from the hatch, which was only just big enough for him to squeeze through, swearing and cursing everything and everybody.

I am sure that he was a clone of Charles Dickens' character Mr Pickwick, when he spoke it was in short sharp sentences with a very high pitched voice. His working attire consisted of a leather skull cap with flaps back and sides, coming down over his shoulders, he always wore a pair of welding goggles with dark green circular lenses, which emphasised his mole like appearance. His jacket was home made from leather, the thickness of which could only have come from a Rhinoceros, it came down below his knees, most of the time hiding a pair of leather knee pads. Below these he wore a pair of leather gaiters that had straps at the back and were specially moulded to encompass his calf muscles, the gaiters fitted over the top of his leather boots which came well up above his ankles, the toe caps were of steel and were scarred by lumps of melted steel that were welded to them, resembling bunches of grapes. His jacket was designed a bit like an old fashioned chauffeurs tunic, with a flap over the front and a high collar. He wore leather gauntlets on his hands which had lift up flaps to expose his first two fingers, enabling him to make the necessary adjustments to his equipment. The whole outfit was impervious to hot sparks and lumps of hot red hot metal, needless to say it was well scorched and battle scared from years of contact with the same.

George was the Graving Docks burner, and he worked with the boiler makers and platers. His skill with an Oxy-Acet'ylene torch was legend, he could burn a hole through a piece of 1 inch thick platework as neat as any drill could cut through. He always had a cigarette in his mouth and rolled his own from a tin which contained the tobacco and a roller arrangement, the paper was put in followed by the tobacco, the lid was shut and the cigarette would pop out from a slot in the lid of the tin. The cigarette that George always had in his mouth, was usually stuck on his lower lip, so that when he spoke it would flap up and down, and as it was rarely longer than an inch, it sometimes disappeared into his mouth like the tongue of a snake. Before commencing to cut metal, he would light up his cutting torch from his flint gun, adjust the flame to the required setting then hold the torch so that the flame was at right angles to his face and light up his cigarette.

After George had pulled himself clear of the hatch, a column of black smoke drifted out of the hole that had been plugged by his body, the shape of which reminded me of a light bulb with legs. He was helped by a group of platers to get well clear of the hatch and they sat him down on some pipework and I could see from where I was standing that he still had his cigarette stuck on his lower lip, I also noticed that smoke was drifting from off of his back. Someone came over with a bucket of water and threw it over him, which turned the smoke into a cloud of steam.

I realised that he had survived a serious injury only because of the type of protective clothing that he wore. He was helped off the ship and sent off to Poplar Hospital on the back of one of the firms lorries that was just leaving for the Royal Albert Dock. I couldn't imagine what they must have thought of him up at the hospital, but I knew from experience that they were used to dealing with all sorts of ship related accidents and all nationalities. George was back at work the next morning, none the worse for his experience, in fact probably better off because of it. Now he would have yet another yarn to spin during tea-breaks, where he always had extraordinary tales to tell, which would leave his captive audience in fits of laughter.

The reason for the explosion was never really solved, it was thought that a pocket of gas had been ignited by George's cutting torch, all the tankers that came up river to be worked on, had their tanks washed out and were gas freed down at Tilbury by the Graving Docks branch of Thames Welding, so in theory they should have been safe to work on.

Advertisement for The Thames Welding Co Ltd. Circa 1959. Thames Welding were part of The London Graving Dock.

Chapter Seven

Tweedy

My time in the fitting shop was coming to an end, the two years had flown by, Big Dave had already left and 'gone outside' so I didn't see much of him. Only when work became a bit slack, or he was working on a ship in the dry-dock, did he manage to pop in and see us, we would then go over to The Gun for a hydraulic lunch and enjoy a couple of pints of their 'Westrams' Best Bitter, unfortunately this ale was discontinued when The Gun came under the Ind Coupe banner.

On reflection I had gained a lot of knowledge, I had mastered the basic skills of filing, marking out and drilling accurately, and I had become confident in the use of the heaviest machine tools that I was ever likely to encounter. From old Jimmy White or 'Whitey' as he was known, I had learnt how to mould and cast white metal bearings, then from old Mac and the rest of the turners I was taught how to machine them, and from Joe McKie how to fit them using hand scrapers that I had made myself. But most of all I had learnt how to respect my fellow workers, all of whom went out of their way to help any apprentice who was willing to learn.

During my last year in the fitting shop, a new apprentice joined us called Jake, he was very cheeky and showed little respect for anyone, this was unfortunate for him as that type of behaviour was not tolerated, especially by the heavy gang, they were the one group of people that you had to keep in with. Somehow Jake upset them, so they kidnapped him and carried him aboard a ship that was in the dry dock, where they put a steel pipe up the sleeve of his boiler suit across his back and out through the other sleeve, he was then hung over the side of the ship on a rope tackle which was attached to the pipe, and left hanging there for the afternoon, with the promise that if he didn't change his attitude he would be left there for the night.

The punishment certainly worked, Jake became a changed person.

Although the heavy gang were classed as labourers, they were perhaps among the most skilled of all the shipyard workers, and in many types of lifting operations, other peoples lives depended on their experience of slinging and handling very heavy and awkward pieces of machinery usually in extremely confined or precarious places. These would include the inside of main engine crankcases, propeller shaft tunnels and high up on stages, set up for the removal of propellers down in the dry-dock.

A few weeks before I was due to go outside, a new turner started work in the fitting shop by the name of Tweedy. Apparently he had never worked in the ship repair industry and came from somewhere outside, because of this, even though he was a first class machinist, he was never really accepted by the old hands. This made me realise how lucky I was to have been given the chance of an apprenticeship in the London Graving Dock Co. where providing you behaved you slowly became accepted as part of a very special community.

One morning after coming out of Blackwall Tunnel on my way to work on my faithful old Norton, I noticed some distance ahead of me 'Tweedy' on his Excelsior auto-cycle; these machines were the fore runner of the mopeds. A heavy bike and grossly under powered by a 98cc Villiers two stroke engine, they also had pedals to assist on hills and for the initial get away if on any sort of incline.

It was a cold wet start to the day and the roads were very slippery, as we came down Cotton Street to the crossing with Poplar High Street, the road here was all cobbles, making it extremely treacherous for anything on two wheels, an old woman stepped out in front of 'Tweedy'. As soon as he applied his brakes the bike slid out from under him and spun round, throwing him clear. Unfortunately by now I was very close, and had no chance of stopping. I knew that if I touched my brakes the same thing would happen to me. I tried to ease the bike over, but couldn't make it and ran right across 'Tweedy's' back wheel, wrecking it completely.

By sheer luck my bike kept upright and I came to a halt on the other side of the cross-roads. I propped the machine up against a wall and went back to see if 'Tweedy' was hurt, when I got to him he was being helped to his feet by a couple of Graving Dock workers and the old woman had made a hasty retreat and disappeared.

Luckily he wasn't injured, only very wet and a bit winded, we carried his auto-cycle off the road and lent it against a shop front. He realised there was nothing either of us could have done to avoid the crash, and was quite good about the fact that I had deprived him of his means of transport to work. I gave him a lift to the yard on the back of the Norton and his bike was later collected by one of the firms lorries and bought back to the fitting shop, where we helped him straighten it up and fit a new back wheel that he had obtained.

Unfortunately having reinstated his means of transport, his luck was to run out again a few days later. One evening, again very wet and by now dark, we were waiting at the far end of the fitting shop alongside the dry-dock for the 5 o'clock whistle to go, this would signal the mad rush down the side of the dry-dock, over the caisson to the timekeepers office to throw our checks in through his window and be off home. I was concentrating on keeping the old Norton's engine running slowly, as it didn't like ticking over, to my right and slightly behind me I could hear 'Tweedy' reving up his Excelsior, which sounded like a ball bearing being rattled in a biscuit tin.

The whistle sounded, and as I went to pull away my engine stopped with the sparking plug oiled up, the rest of the workforce rushed by me, some on push bikes, but most of them on foot. As I lent over to get off the my bike, I looked back and saw 'Tweedy' on his Excelsior flying backwards towards the dry-dock. Luckily for him the dock didn't have a ship in it, and was therefore full of water, I saw him crash through the safety chain that lined the dockside, and disappear over the edge into the dock. Apparently it was possible for these little two stokes to run backwards if they happened to misfire and kick back on being started.

Fortunately a couple of the older hands were still there, so between us we were able to fish him out of the water and get him back into the fitting shop, where he was able to dry his clothes round the coke stoves that Little Arthur had banked up for the night before setting off home. On my way out I told Fred the timekeeper, to let the night-watchman know that 'Tweedy' was still in the fitting shop drying himself off. This was to make sure that he didn't get locked in for the night, because after dark when everyone had left, the place became infested with rats, some of which were of immense size. This was born out by the large amount that Little Arthur caught in his traps every night. The traps were made in the fitting shop from heavy wire, and had a rectangular base with an oval shaped top a bit like an army Nissan hut, they measured about two feet in length and one foot wide, and had heavy steel plate bases. Every morning they would all be full, sometimes two or more in one trap, occasionally he would call us to proudly display one of extraordinary size, before loading them on to a trolley and taking them out to Junction Dock. Once there, he would leave them hanging in the water for most of the day. Sometime during the afternoon he would retrieve them and empty the contents into the dock.

Junction Dock had a peculiar phenomenon that I saw on several occasions, under certain conditions, usually early morning with the sun just breaking through and the mist lifting off the water, the whole dock would turn red, as though it was full of blood. Sometimes it would only last for several minutes and never more than half an hour. If a bucket was scooped in, it would reveal billions of small red worms almost to the consistency of jelly, for some reason they came up to the surface from the silt on the bottom of the dock. It couldn't be proven, but it was generally agreed that it was because of Little Arthur dumping his drowned rats in the dock, that the worms thrived in such vast numbers. I was told by one of the old hands, that before the war the P.L.A. police held their swimming gala in Junction Dock. Although the river was polluted beyond imagination, the West India Dock, by comparison was reasonably clean. This was born out by the fact that when the dry-dock was pumped out, it was quite common to find fish trapped in the drainage gully that ran down the centre of the dock into the sump at the Southern end. On one occasion Sid and I recovered five Roach, two of which were well over a pound in weight, plus a Pike of about five pounds, we returned these to Blackwall Basin just outside the dry-dock, where there must have been a plentyful supply of food for them, least of all the red worms in the adjacent Junction Dock.

This part of The West India Dock system was probably kept in this condition by its comparative isolation from the river, as generally only the locks alongside Aunty Kate's were used, the locks at the Blackwall Basin were rarely used during my time at the Graving Dock, so the area of water consisting of Junction Dock, Blackwall Basin and up into the Import Dock, was hardly disturbed by contact with the river.

While berthed in the enclosed docks all the ships had their toilets locked, so that went a long way in keeping the pollution down, it was a common sight to see the Lascar crews carrying their highly polished two pound jam tins by their improvised wire handles on their way to the toilet block to carry out their ablutions.

'Tweedys' evening swim gave everyone a good laugh the next morning, someone had even left a life jacket and a pair of water wings on his lathe, and one of the fitters told us about the time he was shipwrecked during the war on Henderson Island, also known as Rat Island in the Pacific Ocean. During the day they always kept a look-out from the highest point on the island, one evening the look-out failed to return to camp, on investigation they found him dead at his post, probably from a heart attack, but he had almost been completely eaten by rats.

Poor old 'Tweedy' felt quite ill, and said he wouldn't have stayed behind to dry off if he had heard that story beforehand. The rats were also quite active during the day, they used the overhead rails of the crane to scout along the shop looking for anything consumable, any food such as sandwiches or biscuits had to be kept in a tin, even soap which some hands brought in, had to be sealed away. We kept an air rifle handy, so that at tea breaks we often had a spot of target practice trying to shoot them off the rails, unfortunately it wasn't powerful enough to do any serious damage to them. The best weapon was a catapult, using a large ballbearing or a rusty old nut for ammunition usually did the trick, providing a direct hit was scored. One tea break Joe our fitter, fired at a rat that was sitting on the rail down by Niff-Noffs office, the shot ricocheted and broke one of his windows, we ducked out of site as Niff-Noff appeared at his door, looked at his window then went down and had a go at one of the turners, obviously thinking that a piece of metal had flown from the chuck of his lathe.

As my last week in the fitting shop came to an end, I felt a bit sad about leaving, but I was looking forward to going outside. At last I was going to work on all those magnificent ships that I had first seen all those years ago on my first visit to the docks at the age of seven, when my next door neighbours had taken me with them to meet their son on his return from overseas.

Chapter Eight
Going Outside

On the Monday morning I reported to the outside Foreman, Jack Wandless, who I found in the fitting shop stores, this was the usual congregating place for the work gangs to be organised, prior to going to their respective ships. There was a nucleus of about ten fitters and mates, this would increase as work demanded, about four of these would have an apprentice allotted to them, and provided they got on well, would stay with them until the completion of their apprenticeship. There were also three outside charge hands, who each had a mate known as a runner. His job, was to make sure that the work gangs had everything they needed while on board ship, mainly in the way of small consumables such as, jointing and packing materials, nuts and bolts, etc. They also delivered the wages to the ship on pay-day.

I still didn't know which fitter I would be put with, the ones that I knew, and thought that I would have liked to have gone with, already had an apprentice. As I approached Jack, he was writing something in a small note book, so when he saw me he pointed at me with his pencil and said, "Ah, I've sorted you out, you'll be going with Peter Turner, he's not here at the moment but should be in during the next hour or so, then he's off to a Baron Boat over in the South Dock, she only came in this morning, so hang around and report to him when he gets here."

I had never met Peter before, although I had seen him occasionally in the stores, he was one of the fitters who were nearly always away from the yard, going from one ship to the next and only coming back to the yard to work on a vessel in the dry-dock, or await the arrival of a ship locally in the West India Docks. On the rare occasions that I had seen him, I had never noticed him laughing or joking with the rest of the men, so I began to wonder how we would get on together, and if he was a miserable type of person.

As it turned out, I couldn't have been more wrong, Peter proved to have a wicked and very dry sense of humour. At the end of my apprenticeship I considered myself very lucky and privileged to have been put with him, for not only was he a very skilled fitter he was also a toolmaker, which in those days, before the advent of computer operated machine tools was about as high on the engineering ladder as you could go.

Coincidentally, Peter not only had a new apprentice to contend with that morning, he also had a new fitter's mate, this was Dick Joblin. Dick was in his late fifties, a soft spoken and very strong man, who came from Stepney. He was very efficient as a mate and would always have the correct spanner ready, or obtain any special tools that might be required for some particular job or other.

Before any tools were replaced in the tool box, which was made of steel and about 20 inches long and 12 inches square, he would always clean them so they were free from oil for the next time they were required. This was important, as quite often we would be working high up in the engine room and there was nearly always someone working underneath so it was imperative that no heavy tools were dropped. A large driving spanner, i.e. one that required the use of a heavy hammer to tighten a nut, could inflict a serious injury on anyone below if it slipped or was dropped. Tools of this type were usually secured with a length of cord, if something did fall it would be accompanied by the shout of 'under below' as the object crashed down through the mass of pipes and gratings to land on the engine room plates far below.

Dick would make sure that the tool box was on the lorry ready to go to the relevant ship, where on arrival he would sling it on to his shoulder and carry it up the gangway and down into the engine room, or where ever our job happened to be. I remember on one occasion, for some reason or other he couldn't be there to carry the box on board, so it was left to me to get the tools on the ship. I dragged the box from the back of the lorry onto the tailgate and then slid it on to my shoulder and carried it the few yards to the bottom of the gangway which went up the side of the ship at an angle of about sixty degrees. It was a good two feet to the first step, I suddenly realised that the box seemed to be pushing me down, and it required all my strength to get up on to that first step, before I got half way up my legs turned to jelly and my eyes began to water so that my vision became misty.

I had no idea that a box of that size could be so heavy, it was impossible to put it down as the gangway was too narrow, with my left hand holding the box on my shoulder and using my right hand to pull me up on the rope handrail I struggled on, every step becoming more and more agonising. I remember seeing some people at the top of the gangway waiting to come down, and thinking that I mustn't show any signs of weakness, I just had to keep going. After what seemed a lifetime I made it to the top, the problem now was to get the box from my shoulder to the deck, there was no way I could lower it in a controlled fashion. By a stroke of luck I noticed a companionway leading to the upper deck a short distance ahead, it felt as though my legs didn't belong to me as I staggered towards it in a near state of collapse,

A general engine room view showing the engine tops of a pair of Burmeister and Wain double acting four stroke diesel engines. The engine room plates and control platforms are about 35 feet below the engineers seen in the picture.

but I was able to drop back against the steps and let the box slide backwards onto the nearest step. It took a few minutes to get my breath back, but a good ten more before I had any control over my legs. I carried the box to the engine room entrance, and decided that it was where it was going to stay until Dick arrived, there was no way I could have carried it down all the flights of vertical ladders to the engine room plates far below.

I had seen Dick lift that box on many occasions and sling it up on his shoulder, carry it aboard and take it down into the engine room, sometimes having to negotiate long corridors before finding the engine room door, then carry it down to the bottom of the engine room as though it was no more than a picnic hamper, never once did I hear him mention how heavy it was. I always got on very well with Dick, but after that my estimation of him went right up. When I told him that getting the toolbox on board had nearly beaten me, he laughed and said it wasn't just a case of brute strength, there was a certain knack or skill in lifting heavy objects, plus a fair amount of mental aptitude, as time went on I found out he was right. The three of us got on well together, and I stayed with them for the next three years until the end of my apprenticeship.

My first day with them was more of an adventure than anything else, it was totally different from what I had been doing before. As Dick was already in the stores, Jack introduced us and said that he was sure we would make a good team, while we were talking Peter came in, so Dick went over to him and explained that we were his new boys.

"Right," exclaimed Peter, as he spoke he lightly clapped his hands together and rubbed his palms adding.

"Lets get going, the cars outside and the toolbox is in the boot." We all climbed aboard and sat on the wide bench seat in the front of the car which was an E series Vauxhall Wyvern, with a column gear change. "How about a cup of tea," said Peter as we crossed the bridge and pulled up outside Aunty Kate's. As usual at that time of the morning the place was very busy, Peter opened the door and as we entered the smoke laden interior, he said, "Grab some seats, while I get the teas in."

He returned with the teas, followed by Kate carrying three sausage sandwiches, each one at least three inches thick.

"My treat," said Peter.

In fact both Peter and Dick, would never let me pay for the teas throughout the whole of my three years with them, however they always insisted that I got my round in when we went into a pub for a hydraulic lunch. We left Kate's and drove round to Charlie Brown's entrance at the bottom of the West India Dock Road, this was the heart of what was known as China Town. Charlie Brown's was the name of the pub, just outside the main dock entrance, it was a place with a fearsome reputation, and boxing matches were held there two or three times a week. Boxing was a very popular sport in the area, the other main venue was Poplar Baths in the East India Dock Road.

Several of the older hands at the Graving Dock had been serious fighters in their younger days, and were still highly respected in boxing circles.

One of the most flamboyant of these was Joe, known to everyone as 'Joe Louis,' after the famous world champion from America. Joe originated from Barbados in the West Indies, but had lived in England since before the war. He was the first coloured person that I got to know, and I liked him a lot, as did everyone else in the yard, he had a very friendly and jovial personality that affected everybody in his presence. He went everywhere at a jogging speed, throwing punches at an imaginary opponent along the way, at lunch time he could always be found shadow boxing against a suitable wall or using a skipping rope that had bright red handles, at times reaching phenomenal speeds where his feet became just a blur.

His ears were all twisted and swollen, I never knew what cauliflower ears were until I saw Joe's, his nose was flat against his face, he couldn't have had a bone left in it, and his eyes were just slits in two puffed mounds of flesh. I first met Joe when I was still in the fitting shop, he came jogging down the middle isle punching away at an imaginary opponent, sometimes turning and running backwards. When he noticed me using a hacksaw on a piece of metal in the vice he came over and insisted on showing me how to do it correctly. At first I had difficulty in understanding him, his speech was slurred and as he spoke his tongue seemed to force the words out through his nose. In spite of his condition he still fought bouts at Charlie Brown's. Sometimes, even after 45 years when I pick up a hacksaw in my work shop I can still see him showing me how to use it.

We arrived at the imposing main entrance to the West India Docks and drew alongside one of the P.L.A. policemen on duty, Peter told him who we were, and we were waved through without actually having to stop. We drove round the Eastern end of the Import Dock passing Canary Wharf, then the Export Dock, alongside of which was moored an old torpedo boat, together with one or two other interesting craft, then passing Monkey Island we came to the end of the South Dock, where the General Steam Navigation Company's pleasure boat the Royal Sovereign was just pulling away from her Winter's berth. We then drove down the South side of the South Dock and as we came up between sheds D and C, I could see the name Baron Renfrew, as the bows of our ship came into view. Peter drove round the shed and pulled up at the bottom of the gangway amid a scene of organised chaos. There was a general background noise as the dockside cranes swung about, discharging various commodities from the depths of the ships holds to the waiting gangs of dockers, who eagerly leapt upon the pallets piled high with sacks, of what appeared to be coffee beans, and quickly transferred them to the electric trolleys and sack barrows, they were then taken into the storage sheds to await transhipment.

Then there was the continual clatter of the ships steam winches as they lifted more cargo from the holds, using the derricks to swing it out over the ships side and into lighters which would take it to the up river warehouses. Over all this was the smell of escaping steam coming from the winches and the safety valves, which mixed with the smoke billowing from the black painted top of the funnel, and drifted over the whole area.

Down below in the stokehole, the Donkeyman with only one boiler flashed up, was making sure it was kept 'on the blood' [i.e. the red line on the pressure gauge], which indicates the maximum safe working pressure, to keep the hungry winches fed with steam, much of which was escaping from leaking stuffing boxes and covering the winchmen in clouds of wet condensate. Along the side of the ship, there were various discharges of water and steam, at times the latter drifted up to envelope large areas of the superstructure. Over all this was an unrecognisable aroma, that could only be described as sweet and tangy, that seemed to stick on to your clothing and hair, so that you could still smell it after you got home.

"Get the toolbox and the boiler suits out of the boot, and I'll go and find somewhere out of the way to park the car," said Peter.

"I'll see you up on deck," he added as he drove off.

Dick swung the toolbox up on his shoulder, and I carried the rolled up boiler suits up the gang-way, there was a general vibration and humming sound coming from the depths of the vessel, making it seem as though the ship was alive, and as we waited for Peter to return, an appetising smell drifted out of the adjacent galley where lunch was being prepared for the crew. We watched Peter as he made his way towards the gangway, sometimes dodging out of the way of the constant stream of electric trolleys plying between the ships side and the sheds.

"Something smells good," he said as he joined us on deck. "We'll leave the tools up here and go below and find out what's happening."

The Baron Renfrew was one of H. Hogarth and Sons company's ships, they were generally known as 'Hungry Hogarths,' because of their spartan facilities. It was always difficult to gain access to the engine room stores, so you had to seek out the Donkeyman and persuade him to open up and let you have the required item, such as a length of steam packing, or perhaps a piece of jointing material. If you were successful in getting into the stores, you were only ever given the exact amount, there was never any left over. I never had a meal on any of the Baron Boats, but the food in the galley always looked and smelt good as it was being prepared. Although everything seemed to be run on a shoestring, their ships that I worked on over the years were kept in a good visible sea going condition, and their engine rooms were always tidy and as clean as could be expected.

Chapter Nine

Gilbert

The Baron Renfrew was no exception, she was built in 1935 but was now nearing the end of her days. She was 400 feet long and almost 3700 tons gross, with a speed of 10 knots. With her black hull, and tall buff funnel with a black top, she looked every inch a typical British tramp steamer.

Their latest ships, the Baron Ardrossen and the Baron Ogilvie, which were built in the mid 1950s, were still powered by reciprocating steam engines. they had the latest state of the art superheated triple expansion engines that worked in conjunction with an exhaust turbine that incorporated a reheat system, all their deck machinery and auxiliaries were powered by superheated steam at the full boiler pressure of 220 pounds per square inch.

Peter led the way, and as I stepped over the engine room

H. Hogarth & Sons, 3689 tons gross 'Baron Renfrew' (1935).
Photographed homeward bound in the English channel, heading for London's West India Dock. Photographed by Foto Flite of Ashford, Kent.

door coaming, the heat hit me like an express train. It was so hot, I had difficulty in getting my breath, I followed Peter and Dick down the ladder, finding it impossible to grip the steel hand-rails tightly for more than a few seconds because they were so hot. We reached the cylinder top gratings, and looking down through a maze of pipes and gratings, I could make out people moving about far below on the engine-plates. Peter was already down on the next grating which was level with the main engine crossheads, I quickly followed and arrived down at the engine control platform just behind Dick. It was much cooler down at the bottom of the engine room, there was a lovely smell coming from the steam oil, which in some places such as the piston rods and valve gear was bubbling and hissing from the heat, sometimes making a sound like snapping twigs.

It wasn't too noisy, so it was possible to talk in the normal way, the steam generator was purring away, creating a light vibration which I had felt as we came aboard. Occasionally it would make a loud hissing sound as a stuffing box on one of the piston rods glands leaked a small jet of steam. Above all this was a peculiar noise, which was a cross between a whistle and a moan, that rose and fell at regular intervals. I discovered later that it was coming from the Weirs ballast pump that was transferring water ballast around different parts of the ship to keep her on an even keel, compensating for the cargo that was being discharged from her various holds. This was a noise common to all engine rooms that had steam powered auxiliaries.

Someone came out of the stokehole between the boilers, whom I recognised as George Orbel, he was one of the outside charge hands and he was followed by Freddy Smith who was his runner. George was in charge of the engineering work being carried out on the Baron Renfrew and it was his responsibility to make sure that everything was done properly and on time. He came over to Peter and said that there were two jobs for us to be getting on with, one was a steam valve chest on the boiler tops, and the other was one of the boiler feed pumps in the engine room. He asked where our tools were and Peter told him that we had left them up on deck until we found out what the situation was.

"That's ok then, you can take them in through the fidley and strip out the valve chest first, I'll check with the second engineer and make sure all the lines are shut down," said George.

Peter explained how important it was to make sure that all the live steam valves in the line that we were going to work on were shut, and all their handles tied with cord.

A year or so later I saw the horrific results of a failure to observe this precaution, a fitters mate had his face burnt off, because one of the ships engineers opened a live steam valve while the fitters mate was working on a valve chest. We climbed back out of the engine room, Dick picked up the tool box and we followed Peter to the base of the funnel just in front of the engine room skylights. Here there was another door that led onto a grating at the very top of the stokehole, just inside, a two cylinder steam engine was purring away, driving a fan, which was supplying air down to the boilers. This area was known as the Fidley and from here a series of ladders and gratings went right down to the stokehole plates.

It was very gloomy inside, with only the odd light bulb emitting a dim yellow glow here and there. Peter found the valve chest that we had to overhaul, it was right on top of one of the boilers.

"See if you can find some cord to lash the valves with, try the fo'castle don't bother with the stores its bound to be locked," he shouted across to me from out of the gloom. As I climbed up towards the boat deck I heard him shout again.

"Watch out for the Bo'sun."

I was just bending over to get out on deck, when I was suddenly pushed forward by something jumping on my back, whatever it was lept off just as quickly. I looked back into the gloom of the fidley for sometime but couldn't see anything, I could hear Peter saying something to Dick right down on the boiler tops, so it I new it wasn't either of them messing around. I could still feel the place on my back where whatever it was had hit me, and as I made my way forward dodging the pallets of cargo being swung out of the holds it suddenly dawned on me that it must have been the ship's cat. I managed to get past No.1 hatch in one piece and entered the fo'castle, to my left was a large teak door that was slightly open, I gave it a push and stepped over the coaming and went inside.

While I was trying to get accustomed to the darkness, there was only a single light bulb in the far corner, which couldn't have been more than 20 Watts, I was almost overcome by the strong damp smell of tar and hemp rope, with a mixture of paint and red lead thrown in. I then received my second fright of the day, thinking the fo'castle was deserted, I was about to have a look around for some suitable cord, when a deep voice with a strong Scottish accent suddenly boomed out from somewhere in shadows.

"There's nothing here worth stealing, what are you after?"

This was probably the Bo'sun, I thought to myself, I've got to get on the right side of him, if I am going to make a good impression with Peter by returning with some sort of cord.

"Good morning Bo'sun, I didn't see you over there, you gave me quite a start, in fact its the second fright I've had in the last few minutes," I answered, trying to put over a friendly tone of voice. I heard him grumble some remark from the darkness, and as I still couldn't see him, I felt my way in the general direction of where his voice came from, telling him how I had been attacked by the ships cat as I came out of the fidely.

"Och that'll nae be the ships cat, because we have nae got one, that would have been Gilbert, he's a vicious little beastie, ye dunae want to get near him," he said in a warning manner. "Who's Gilbert?" I asked

"Och he's some sort of monkey, the Donkeyman got him on the African coast, but he escaped and has made his home in the stokehole, he regards it as his territory and does nae like anyone going up there," he replied. He went on to tell me that all the engineers were frightened to go up on the boiler tops, as Gilbert would leap out of the dark onto their heads, apparently the third engineer had been bitten on his ear during the voyage, and it was now quite badly infected, and the Captain had offered a reward for Gilbert's capture.

I seemed to be getting on quite well with the old Bo'sun, he had come over from where he had been splicing a heavy wire rope, by now my eyes had become accustomed to the semi darkness and I could see that he was in his sixties, he may have been older, but it was difficult to tell as he had a large grey moustache and beard which blended with his grey hair, that showed from beneath a well worn, blue woolly hat. I thought I would take a chance and ask him for some cord.

"I've come up to see if I could scrounge a length of twine to tie off some live steam valves on the boiler tops," I ventured to ask him.

I was very surprised when he replied,

"Och nae bother, I'll see what I can find."

As he spoke he lifted a clay pipe off a rack and proceeded to light it up. When he had it well alight, and amid clouds of creamy smelling smoke, that I recognised as a Dutch tobacco, he began rummaging about amongst a selection of large paraffin navigation lights. He then came over to me carrying two lamps, each had a length of hard oily rope trailing from their handles, producing a small knife from a sheath on his belt, he cut the lengths of rope from the handles and handed them to me.

"Mind you bring them back when you have finished, otherwise we'll both be in trouble, Lampy does nae like anyone interferring with his gear," he said in a threatening manner. Many ships still carried a lamp trimmer, they were usually old shellbacks who had been to sea all their lives, and seemed to keep themselves to themselves, as nobody ever knew where their cabins were, they were always difficult to make contact with, it was their job to maintain all the ships oil lamps and to help the Bo'sun when required. Their tiny workshop was usually to be found in part of one of the deck houses, and it was always kept locked. To catch a glimpse of a Lampy was like spotting a creature that was thought to be extinct.

I thanked the Bo'sun and assured him I would return the cord, and beat a hasty retreat from the fo'castle, where I was momentarily dazzled by the bright daylight outside. I had to stop for a while to judge when it was safe to make my way back along the deck without being knocked over by the slings of cargo being craned out of the holds. It was impossible to run as the decks were obstructed by piles of hatch boards, wire strops, and dunnage [Lengths of timber].

When I rejoined Peter and Dick, I found them both covered in a coating of white asbestos flock. This had come from the lagging which had covered the valve chest, they had to break it away with a heavy screwdriver and a small crowbar to expose the nuts and bolts on the pipe flanges. Peter then explained that he had removed one of the valve covers and found the seat too badly worn away to repair on site, so that the whole valve chest would have to be stripped out and sent ashore to the fitting shop. I gave Peter the rope, which had left my hands sticky and smelling of tar, and he indicated for me to follow him along the grating, pointing out the steam line that was shut down. We clambered over the top of the starboard boiler to a large valve.

"Right this is one of the stop valves that have been shut down, I'll leave you to tie the handle while I go and do the other one, I'll see you back at the valve chest," he remarked.

As he was leaving I told him to watch out as there was a monkey on the loose in the stokehole. He turned round with a start, "Did you say monkey," his face looked whiter than the asbestos that covered his hair. I then went on to tell him of my encounter with some sort of creature as I left the fidely, and that the Bo'sun had told me it was a monkey called Gilbert, with a price on his head, belonging to the Donkeyman. As I spoke Peters eye brows went up above his horned rimmed spectacles, and his mouth widened into a smile of anticipated mischief. This was an expression that I got to know over the years, as it always for warned me that he had some sort of trick up his sleeve, and from that first time I saw him use it I knew we were going to get on well.

"I hate monkeys, I once got grabbed by Guy the gorilla up at London Zoo, it was only by luck that I never lost my arm." Half way through telling me this a flake of asbestos fell off his forehead onto the end of his nose, which he blew off, using his lower lip to direct the blow.

"Lets go and find the Donkeyman!" he said.

We climbed down the ladders to the bottom of the stokehole, where I found it was much cooler, it was also deserted, except for a person in a blue overall jacket with trousers to match, the same sort of thing that steam locomotive drivers wore. He was bending over looking through a small apperture into the furnace of the boiler that was flashed up, and at the same time he was making slight adjustments to the fuel valve on the furnace front. Peter went along to him and spoke for a few minutes, the man pointed up to the mass of pipework and gratings that we had just emerged from and moved his arm in an arc, then shrugged his shoulders. They then shook hands, and as Peter came back I noticed that the man, who turned out to be the Donkeyman was looking at us with a big smile and slowly shaking his head. As Peter reached me, he clapped his hands, and as he rubbed them together, he said with that smile, that I got to know so well,

"Its about dinner time, let's go and find Dick, if we get going now we should get a table at 'Kettles,' then we've got some shopping to do."

As we went out of the stokehole between the boilers and into the engine room, Peter shouted across to George the charge hand, who was leaning over talking to one of the other fitters, who was down in the crankpit of the main engine.

"We're off to lunch."

George looked up, and stretched out his arm with his thumb raised and gave a nod. We climbed up the series of ladders, through the heat barrier and emerged into the sunlight. After removing our boiler suits, and hanging them on the handrail just inside the engine room, we made our way down the gangway, and as it was a warm sunny day we didn't need our coats. As we reached the bottom of the gangway, Peter said,

"We'll leave the car and walk round, I don't want to loose my parking spot, it was getting busy with lorries when I left it there this morning."

It was only a ten minute walk to the main gate, and there was so much to see, the dock was nearly full with ships from all parts of the world. Kettle's cafe was just a few doors up from Charlie Brown's, behind its dingy exterior could be had some of the finest dinners in the area. Their speciality being individual steak and kidney puddings; known locally as babies heads. Kettle's also had some special way of boiling potatoes, no matter what season, they were always had a perfect creamy texture, because of this it was difficult to get a table after 12:30. They also had a tea machine, similar to the one in Farina's at Blackwall, where a dozen cups of tea could be dispensed at one time. Having finished our dinners, Peter said,

"There's no time for cards today, we've got work to do."

He then went back to the counter and had a word with one of the staff, who then bent down behind the counter and came up holding two milk bottles, one was a pint, the other a quart size, [twice the size of a pint], and handed them across to Peter. We then left Kettles, and crossed the West India Dock Road, and went down Pennyfields into the centre of China Town, the shops in this area were all owned by Chinamen, and in many cases were a front for the Opium Dens and Fan Tan clubs that gave this area its dubious reputation. However at that time of day it all looked quite normal, the only difference being the Chinese writing on the shop fronts.

These places were sometimes raided by the police, without success, as the Chinese had an early warning system, second to none, which gave them time to disappear without trace. The secret of their ability to do this was revealed when the area was later bulldozed to the ground, to make way for a new development. It was not uncommon to see a J.C.B. nose dive into a large void, the whole area resembled a rabbit warren of underground passageways, interconnecting all the properties.

We stopped outside a Chinese Greengrocers, and waited while Peter went in taking the milk bottles with him. He was in there for some time, eventually emerging carrying a small brown paper bag, with the opening rolled up so that we couldn't see its contents.

"Right lets get back aboard, that took longer than I thought, they were playing 'Mah-Jong' in the back room, I could hear them rattling the tiles, the world stops for them when they start playing that game," said Peter.

As we returned via Ming Street, Dick asked Peter what he was up to.

"We could be on to an earner, all will be revealed when we get back to the stokehole," replied Peter, tapping the end of his nose.

We were soon back at the ship, but before going up the gangway, Peter asked me to see if I could find a couple of empty sacks over in the sheds across the quay, and bring them down into the fidely, to the valve chest that we were stripping out. This proved to be no problem, as there was a large pile of them just outside 'D' shed. I selected two good ones, and set off back aboard, completely baffled by what Peter was up to. I rejoined the pair of them on the grating over the boiler, carrying the sacks rolled up under my arm. Peter looked up and said.

"Ah you've got the sacks, well done Dave, right here's what we're going to do; apparently there's a £10 reward for the monkey's capture, I've also got a fiver bet on with the Donkeyman that we can catch the bloody thing, that makes it fifteen quid, or a fiver each when we get him, as I don't know how big it is, I've got two different sized milk bottles. We'll tie the small one to the handrail and leave the big one on that grating at the top of the fidely." He then produced a selection of nuts from the brown paper bag saying,

"I picked these out in the Chinaman's so that they just fit in the neck of the milk bottles, there's half a dozen small ones for the pint one, and the same amount of larger ones for the quart bottle."

After sorting out the nuts, he put them into the appropriate bottles and then said,

"You have to make sure that you leave a nut half in the spout, so that when the monkey goes to grab it, it drops into the bottle. That way he will put his arm into the bottle and grab one of the nuts inside, once he's got hold of one he won't let go. With his hand round one of the nuts it will be too big to come out of the bottle, we then get one of these sacks over him, tie up the opening, then put the lot into the other sack just to make sure, and we've all made a good days wages."

Dick and I followed Peters instructions with a certain amount of doubt.

"What makes you think this is going to work," said Dick.

"I've seen monkeys caught out in India like this, so if it works for Indian monkeys, it should work for African ones," replied Peter, as he carefully placed a nut in the neck of the pint bottle. We soon had the bottles set up in what seemed likely places, and it was soon time to return to work. We continued to remove the nuts and bolts from the flanges of the valve chest, most of which had to be split off with a hammer and chisel. At about 3 o'clock George the charge-hand came up to see how things were going.

"Looks like you'll soon have it free, I'll get the heavy gang to get it ashore, apparently they're going to work all night on it in the fitting shop, so we should have it back in the morning. There's a turn going tonight, so if you want you can strip out the feed pump," he said.

A turn meant working until 9pm, that was four hours overtime at double time, making eight hours extra pay, plus the P.B.R. bonus, that now, as I was working outside I was entitled to, add to that the fiver reward if we caught the monkey, which in itself was more than a weeks wages to me; it all sounded too good to be true. We soon had the valve chest ready to go ashore, so we left it to the heavy gang, and climbed down to the stokehole and went through into the engine room to make a start on the feed pump. It was much cooler down at plate level, and much brighter, there was also a lot of activity going on, the end cover of the main engine condenser had been removed to enable some leaky tubes to be plugged, also the bottom end bearing of the H.P. cylinder had been removed for inspection.

Peter then told me that we should have the feed pump all stripped out by 6pm ready for the surveyor to inspect in the morning, so that all being well we should be away by

6:15. Things were really looking good, my first day outside, earning more money than ever before, and going home at 6:15 and being paid till 9:00pm.

I soon became aware that this was how things were done, providing that the job was on time, and if the amount of work set down for that day was completed in the time allowed for it, in the overtime given, then all hands would slip away home; this was known as 'Hoppy Hoppy'. All this was possible because when working out of the yard, there was no official clocking on or off. Peter was right in his estimation, we were able to get away just after six, but as we were not in luck, so far as the capture of Gilbert was concerned, Peter said that we had better cover over the bottles with rags, as we did not want the monkey getting trapped while we were ashore, someone else might find him and claim the reward. That morning being unsure where I would be going, I left the Norton at home, and came by bus, so when Peter offered me a lift as far as Charlton, I readily accepted. I then caught a bus and was home by 7:15, all in all, my first day outside had gone very well, I had even learnt how to catch a monkey, in theory at least!.

The next morning I boarded the Baron Renfrew at 8am, put on my boiler suit, which had been kept nice and warm on the handrail at the top of the engine room, and went below, there I found Peter and Dick sitting on some large valve handles talking together, Peter was just finishing a cigarette.

He told me that he had uncovered the traps, so all we had to do was to keep our ears open. George came over and told us that the valve chest was coming aboard. As he was speaking, I realised what Peter had meant about keeping our ears open.

Suddenly, from the stokehole there came an ear piercing screech.

"Got the bastard," shouted Peter, as his eyebrows went up, he beamed a big smile. We all rushed through into the stokehole, George having no idea what was going on, thought that someone had been seriously injured. The screeching was coming from up on the boiler tops, George shouted that he would go and phone for an ambulance.

"No need for that, its only Gilbert, quick Dave get the sacks," said Peter.

"Who the bloody hell's Gilbert?" asked George as we climbed up the ladders to the top of the boilers. We reached the pint bottle, to find Gilbert with his arm inside, still screeching and showing all his teeth in a wide grin like expression.

"Right get the sack over him and make sure that as I cut the bottle free, it all goes in the sack," said Peter.

All went according to plan, we managed to tie up the end of the sack, and put the whole lot into the second sack that Dick was holding open. We were just tying up the second sack when George arrived, still wanting to now what it was that we had got.

"Its a nice little bonus," Peter told him.

We carried the sack, which by now had gone quiet, out of the fidely and on to the deck. Peter told me to go and find the Donkeyman as quickly as possible, and to tell him to fetch the reward and our winnings with him.

I found the Donkeyman in his cabin and gave him the message.

"How the hell did you catch him, we have tried everything to get the little bastard, I'll have to get the reward money from the Chief Engineer," he said with a look of complete amazement on his face.

I told him that we were up on the boat deck by the funnel, and would wait for him to arrive. I then returned to Peter saying that the Donkeyman had gone to get the reward money from the Chief.

"Right you stay here and look after Gilbert, me and Dick will go and make a start boxing up the valve chest, give us a shout when he arrives," he said.

Gilbert had gone very quiet, there was no movement from the sack, and I was beginning to wonder if he was still alive. After about twenty minutes the Donkeyman arrived in company with the Chief and Second engineer.

"So you've got the little blighter then," exclaimed the Chief, "Lets have a look at him," he added.

As he picked up the sack, Gilbert started screeching and throwing himself about, at least he was still alive I thought to myself.

"Perhaps not," said the Chief, quickly setting the sack down.

I shouted down the fidely to Peter, who came up with Dick, the Chief then handed the ten pounds to Peter, saying, "What do we do with him now."

"I've no idea, I only catch em, I don't keep em," answered Peter, who then looked across at the Donkeyman and said, "I believe you owe me five pounds."

The Donkeyman produced a handful of pound notes, and begrudgingly counted out five of them into Peters outstretched hand.

"Well we'll leave you with Gilbert, we've got work to do," he said as he turned round and went back into the stokehole; Dick and I followed. As we climbed down to the valve chest to do up the last few bolts, before getting the steam turned on to test for leaks, Peter said with a big smile,

"Wait till they find the milk bottle stuck on Gilbert's arm, they'll have to break it to get it off, I'd like to be a Gunnel Fly when they try."

We finished boxing up the pipe flanges on the valve chest, using new gaskets that I had knocked out of a sheet of steam jointing (my first outside job). Cutting gaskets from this material can be painful as it is reinforced with fine wire that always seems to pierce down your finger nails. I untied the handles of the steam valves further up the line, taking care to look after the cord, then I went below to find the 4th engineer who was on duty to ask him to turn on the steam. He came straight up and cracked open the valves, so that we could check for leaks. Peter told us to keep well back, just to be on the safe side as a steam leak could cause a serious injury, he announced that all was well, and then said that it must be time for a tea break.

Chapter Ten

The Mobiles

"We'll go to the Mobile, it should be here about now," he said, looking at his wristwatch that he had taken from his pocket. The Mobiles were run by the P.L.A. canteen service, and consisted of a fleet of especially converted vans that operated within the dock system, they had a drop down side that served as a counter once they arrived at their station. They usually had a crew of two women, one took care of the tea's and coffee and the other looked after the food. By the nature of the environment they had to have a sense of humour, the good natured banter from their motley assortment of customers washed over them like water off a ducks back. They stopped at various places on the quayside for the stevedores and other dockworkers to get a cup of tea in the mornings and afternoons. It was always good practice, when you started on a ship, to ask the quayside workers when the Mobile was due, that way you wouldn't miss it. Just as in the main P.L.A. canteens, where the tea and coffee tasted much the same, so it was with the Mobiles, the only noticeable difference being the price. They mainly sold bread rolls, of which there were two choices, roll and butter or roll with cheese. The rolls were always the crusty type, the crust was usually burnt almost black and could be pulled off in one piece like a shell. The only way to tackle it, was to dunk it in the large china mug of tea or coffee to soften it up. In spite of these small criticisms the Mobiles were a welcome site when they turned up on the quay, more so in Winter, especially if you happened to be working out on deck, overhauling a steam winch. We worked on the Baron Renfrew for the rest of the week, this meant that I would receive a bonus payment about four weeks later. It usually took that long after a ship was finished for the office to work out what percentage of standard rate of pay, we would receive. On average it probably worked out at about 35%.

After the Baron Renfrew, we worked on a variety of ships,

sometimes steam powered, usually with triple expansion main engines, occasionally turbine driven vessels, such as Ellerman's, 7063 tons 'City of Lyons' which was built in 1926. Ellerman's were one of the Graving Docks main customers.

Many of their ships were diesel powered, Doxfords being the predominant engine installations. Port line was another company we frequently did work for, the majority of their ships were powered by twin engined diesels.

Over the years we also worked on many of Harrison's ships such as, 'Student,' 'Successor,' and the 'Prospector,' all of which were known as 'Sam Boats,' these were powered by triple expansion engines, in a very basic engine room. They were built during the war, and were not expected to survive many voyages, for this reason they were very spartan in their accommodation, and engine installation.

However many did survive the war, and continued to trade right through the 1950s and into the 1970s. The engineers on these Harrison vessels always kept the engine rooms in a clean and tidy condition and I always found it a pleasure to work on them. Under the Harrison flag they traded extensively from the U.K. to the West Indies, East and West

Harrison Lines 1943 Historian. (7262) tons gross.
One of the many 'Liberty' ships known as 'Sam' Boat that the writer worked on, usually while berthed in West India Docks South Quay, or 'Rum Quay' as it was locally known.

Africa, and across the Indian Ocean to India and Ceylon.

Their later ships, such as the 'Governor,' 'Diplomat,' and 'Astronomer,' were motor vessels with Doxford main engines, which were probably the most common of the diesels that we worked on. They were favoured by many ship owners, because of their comparative simplicity, giving them reliability and economy.

Chapter Eleven

The Link One

One morning we reported to the stores, to be told that we had a job on a ship called the 'Link One,' a vessel of about 2000 tons that was laying in the river Medway just off Rochester down in Kent. This was the furthest that we had ever travelled to work on a ship; work in that area would normally be carried out by the Graving Docks Tilbury yard. We did however sometimes work in the Tilbury Docks, and the various jetties on the North bank of the river, such as Pheonix Wharf on Frog Island at Rainham, this was a very remote jetty, only accessible by a narrow gauge industrial railway, that hauled timber from the jetty to the timber yards. When working at Pheonix Wharf we would have to load all our gear, plus ourselves on to one of the wagons and travel the mile or so down to the jetty by rail.

On these remote wind swept jetties any deck work, such as steam winches and windlass's was usually given to the apprentices to carry out. It was a nice job during the summer, but in the depths of winter it was hard going, especially fitting and scraping in new bearings on a windlass right up on the fo'castle in the face of ice cold sleet, driven by an Easterly gale.

The other jetties where we occasionally went were Fords motor works, at Dagenham Dock, and the jetty at Purfleet, where we would work on the oil tankers that discharged there. On occasions we had to reach these places by train, using the main line to Tilbury, the carriages on this line were in a filthy condition and hauled by a steam tank locomotive, known locally as the 'Tilbury Flyer,' which was a contradiction in terms as it must have been the slowest train in the country.

Another jetty that we sometimes went to, was across the river at Northfleet, this was at Bowater's paper works, where we worked on their own ships, such as the 6471 ton 'Sarah

Bowater,' and the 4045 ton 'Elizabeth Bowater,' just two of the ships that made up their fleet of about ten vessels during the late 1950s. These ships carried pulp for newsprint from Canada and Newfoundland to Bowaters own paper plants.

The job that we had to do on the 'Link One' was to rebore the H.P. [high pressure] cylinder on the main engine, we were given the job, because Peter was the only one that had ever used the boring machine before, and that was some years previously. The Foreman told us to find the boring gear, which was somewhere in the stores, even Fred the storekeeper had lost track of it, and give it all a good service and make sure it was all there, so that it could be taken down to Rochester the next morning on the lorry. Peter described what it looked like and we began searching for it among all the various boxes of rarely, or ever used equipment which was piled high at the back of the stores.

It took us an hour or more before Dick found a sack, covered in a thick layer of dust, the contents of which Peter was able to confirm as being something to do with boring gear. Further rummaging through the piles of sacks full of special jigs and apparatus, brought to light what seemed to be the complete contraption.

We laid it all out on the floor of the stores, and Peter showed us how it all went together. There were two adjustable three pronged spreaders that fitted top and bottom of the cylinder, a large screwed rod that went between them in a special tube, and a boring bar that rotated down the screwed rod, cutting the cylinder wall to the required depth. All this was driven by a flat belt from an old remotely mounted electric motor. It was all very old and looked like a heap of scrap iron from the Victorian era. After we had given it a good clean up and checked that the electric motor, along with everything else still worked, we laid it all out ready to be loaded on the lorry.

The next morning, having been given the necessary directions the day before, I set off to find the ship on my old Norton. It usually took me over an hour to get to the West India Docks in the mornings on the bike, this was due to the heavy traffic congestion, especially in the Blackwall Tunnel area, as the crow flies, it was only a distance of about four miles. Rochester on the other hand was some thirty miles away, but the route was mainly on the A2 so I was able to get the Norton on 'full song' and arrived down at Rochester in less than forty minutes.

I found the jetty where it was arranged that we would be picked up by a launch and taken out to the ship, which was tied up to Buoys some way down river. I found a suitable place to leave the bike, and went into a nearby cafe for a cup of tea and await the arrival of Peter and Dick. It was not long before the Vauxhall pulled up at the riverside, I had a good view from where I was sitting in the cafe, so when they arrived I ordered the teas and went out and gave them a shout. They came over and Peter remarked that we ought to come this way more often, it being such a pleasure not to get stuck in traffic for hours on end in the dock area's. He said that he knew that I would be here, as I had passed him going like a bat out of hell across Dartford Heath, I had to admit that I hadn't seen them.

There were dark clouds looming as far as the Norton was concerned, there was talk of a roadworthy test being introduced for vehicles over ten years old. This would mean that there was no hope for me to be able to use the bike in its present state, as it was a pure racing machine, with no provision for electric's such as lights and things. I had fitted lamps from a push bike, but they wouldn't pass any official examination, so it looked as though her road going days were numbered, especially as I didn't feel inclined to seriously modify the machine by fitting a dynamo and all the necessary bits and pieces. We were talking about this over our teas, when Peter said, "It seems to me, you'll have to pass your test and get a car. As it happened his idea had been in the back of my mind for some time, it began when, one day I pulled into a garage to fill up the Norton with petrol.

Parked over to one side was their breakdown truck, it was the type that had been converted from a large car and had a small crane on the back for hitching up broken down vehicles. I pulled up along side it and realised

111

that it was a Rolls-Royce, the whole vehicle was in an immaculate condition, with a polished aluminium bonnet of extraordinary length, the interior of the open cab was polished in the same way, the instruments were right down under the scuttle and were a magnificent display of how things should be done. While I was drooling over the Roll's, a mechanic came over and did the same thing with the Norton.

"Make a nice pair don't they," he remarked.

I had to agree, but the Rolls Royce had something about it that put it into a class of its own. He lifted the bonnet to show me the engine, which seemed a mass of polished copper and brass, and gave me the impression of a small marine engine. While I was looking under the bonnet, he told me that it was a 1914 Silver Ghost, and that they had converted it into a breakdown truck some years previously, after the original bodywork had been destroyed by a small tree falling on it. I said that if ever I became rich, I would most certainly get one like it. He then said something that I found hard to believe.

"You don't have to be rich, you can pick up these old Rolls Royce's from about £50, that's the going rate for them in most scrap yards." He then shut the bonnet and gave the silver lady mascot a twist so that it faced forward and said.

"When you get one, make sure you always remember to turn the mascot, otherwise you'll damage the bonnet as you open it, get yourself a copy of 'Motor-Sport' and look up the adverts, nobody wants em! especially with the ten year test coming up and all the recent petrol rationing due to the Suez crisis."

The following week I visited the library at Poplar Technical College and looked at the motoring magazines, sure enough there were several Rolls Royce's for sale between £95 and £120, and if the photographs were anything to go by, they looked to be in nice condition. I considered that I had discovered one of the best kept secrets of the motoring world.

"Ah looks like that's our launch coming in," said Peter.

We left the cafe and strolled down to the jetty, timing it so that we arrived just as it was coming alongside.

"Going out to the Link One," Peter asked the skipper.

"That's right jump aboard," he replied.

The launch then backed out into the river without having to tie up, the skipper then manoeuvred it round into the current, and we were soon heading out to the ship.

"We'll go aboard and look things over, and make a start, stripping out the H.P. [high pressure] piston while we wait for the lorry to get here," said Peter, as he tried to get some shelter from the spray that was starting to come over the bows.

The launch came up alongside the ships gangway, where we were able to jump across on to the boarding platform while the skipper kept the launch stemming the tide. When we went below to the engine room we found that the ships engineers had already removed the H.P. cylinder cover, so we were able to see the damage to the cylinder wall, which was probably caused by lack of oil or a broken piston ring. It wasn't too hot on the cylinder tops, so that made things much more comfortable for working.

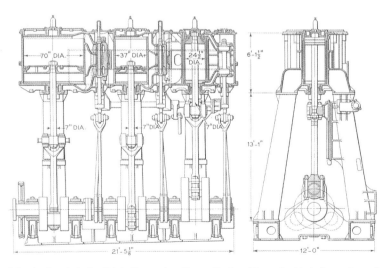

A basic drawing of a Triple Expansion Steam Engine (Three Legger). An engine of these dimensions would develop around 2500 H.P. and would be fitted to a ship such as the 'Baron Renfrew' referred to in chapter nine.

Peter asked me to go below and make sure that the turning gear was fully engaged, there was a notice hanging on the main steam stop valve, that said it was, never the less, for our own safety, we always liked to make sure.

Should the propeller turn while we were working on any of the reciprocating parts of the main engine, it could mean serious injury or even death, if the crankshaft moved unintentionally. This could easily happen when the tide was running fast while the ship was tied up to buoys, as the pressure of water on the blades of the propeller could cause it to turn without warning. The other dangers were from floating logs, small craft, or barges hitting the propeller.

Later during my apprenticeship, one of the Scalers, [these were the cleaners who performed all the dirtiest jobs that could be imagined, and many more that couldn't in the ship repair yards], was in the process of cleaning out the scavenge trunking of a large diesel engine. The trunking was large enough for a man to crawl through, and the inside would be coated with a layer of black oily, tar like deposit that could only be removed by the use of hand scrapers.

As he put his arm through the inlet port to remove some lumps of scavenge residue, that had dropped onto the piston crown, a barge drifted against the propeller, causing it to kick the engine the engine round sufficiently, that the piston came up and sheared off his arm. It was impossible to hear his screams from outside the engine, so he was left to his own devices to extricate himself from the terrible situation that he found himself in. His awful plight wasn't discovered until he reached the access panel in the trunking several yards away, where his cries for help were eventually heard.

He was taken to Poplar Hospital, covered in a thick coating of black oil, mixed with the blood that had poured from what was left of his arm. As no one was prepared to crawl back through the trunking, the exhaust piston had to be craned out to gain access to the top of the lower piston, to retrieve his severed arm.

One of the things that Peter instilled in me was the safety aspect regarding working on board ship. When working down in the engine room of an unfamiliar vessel we always checked our escape routes and the whereabouts of the fire extinguishers before commencing any work. One of these routes was the tunnel escape, this was accessed at the stern of the engine room via the water tight door between the engine room and the propellor shaft tunnel. We always made a point of wedgeing open the door so that it couldn't be shut while we were down below. If the ship had a fire drill the water tight door would be shut as part of the drill, this was done from the top of the engine room by turning a large hand wheel which was connected to the door by a series of articulated rods. The other main escape route was through boiler room and up out of the fidly, so we always made sure that the door to the deck was secured open.

The main danger was from fire, the others were from serious steam leaks, crankcase explosions and the odd diesel generator that ran away. The latter could have serious consequences should it ever occur. It happened to one of the firms lorry's while in the yard, it slowly increased in rev's until the engine disintegrated. On another occasion a ship in the dry dock at The Royal Albert Dock had one of its generators run away, the 5th engineer tried to stop it by holding down the control lever, but it was to no avail! Even with the fuel cut off, the rev's continued to increase alarmingly as it drew up the lubricating and used it as fuel. The flywheel suddenly exploded into many pieces, one lump sliced the cheek off the behind of the engineer and another ripped through the ships side and ended up on the bottom of the dry dock. If it had happened at sea the ship would have been in serious trouble.

Some years later I experienced a similar occurrence outward bound to New Zealand. In mid Atlantic I was asleep in my bunk when I was awoken by a terrific vibration, it seemed as though my cabin was being shaken by a giant fist. The engine room alarm started ringing in the alleyway outside and all the off watch engineers rushed down the engine room which was full of thick smoke. When I reached the engine room plates I could find no trace of the 4th and 7th engineers who were on watch, I rushed round the starboard side of the main engine to be confronted with a huge ball of fire coming from the armature of one of the generators. Luckily a large fire extinguisher was nearby, I was just getting it going when all the lights went out, leaving only the great ball of flame as illumination. While I was dealing with the fire the main engine slowed down and stopped, it later transpired by the chief. As all the main engine auxiliaries such as lubricating oil pumps were driven by electric motors a serious catastrophe was avoided.

The engine had been revolving so fast that all the white metal bearings had run and the top end bearings had become red hot and split the cylinder liners so that all the cooling water poured in and filled up the sump. All the push rods shot into the air above the engine, some hitting pipes and valves badly bending the rods (these push rods were about one and a quarter inches in diameter).

I managed to put out the fire, at the same time as the lights came on, it was then that I saw the 4th and 7th engineers who had been trapped behind the great ball of flame. Except for thinking their number was up, they were quite unharmed. We discovered that the start of all the trouble was caused by a broken spring in the governor, the engine then raced away, causing the polarity to change on the electric control board, so that the dynamo became the driving force and drove the diesel engine to destruction.

In spite of the severity of the breakdown, we went onto six hour watches and rebuilt the engine from spare parts and fitted a new armature that had been secured to the engine room casing right up at the top of the engine room. The operation to get the armature down to the bottom of the engine room and round to the other side of the main engine, necessitated the removal of access ladders and a large amount of pipework, some of which had to be by passed. It also required the combined efforts of the deck crew and the engineers to lower it down, as the armature was secured higher than the overhead engine room crane. This was done using the deck winches via suitably placed snatch blocks and a series of signals. By the time we reached Panama the generator was running and back on load.

I reported back to Peter that all was O.K. with the turning

gear, so we went down to the middle platform and started disconnecting the piston rod from the crosshead, after which we were able to hoist out the piston and rod using the ships overhead lifting gear. The H.P. piston was only 450mm in diameter so we didn't need the services of the heavy gang, we were just finishing when we were told that the lorry had arrived with the gear, so we went off in the launch to unload it and fetch it aboard.

When we came ashore, we were greeted by Big Arthur who had now joined the heavy gang, he had been sent down on the lorry to give us a hand. After we unloaded the lorry, Peter took us all back into the cafe, where he treated everyone to a mug of tea and a sausage sandwich. It wasn't long before we were on our way back to the ship, where with Big Arthur to help us, the gear was soon lowered down into the engine room through the skylight. It took the rest of the afternoon to set it all up and make sure it was all running true, ready to start the actual reboring the next morning. Peter estimated that it would take about two hours to do one complete cut, so as we didn't want to stop halfway through a cut, he said we might as well go home. We left the ship just before 6pm, and I was home by 6:30, my mother wondered what had happened, as I never arrived home before 7pm.

The next morning we were on board by 8:30, having started the machine, we had to watch it closely to make sure everything was going to plan, Peter asked me to find a sheet of canvas and hang it under the cylinder, so as to catch the swarf, [cuttings] as the boring bar made its agonisingly slow progress down the cylinder on its trial run. It took two and a quarter hours to do one cut, slightly more than Peter had thought, so that meant we would be able to do four cuts during the day, provided the gear held up. After the first cut Peter suggested that we work a rotor system, so that two of us could go ashore, while two stayed to keep an eye on things. The system worked well, after each cut the boring bar was adjusted by whoever was there, so that it was in continual motion all day and we all had a chance to go ashore for a pint or two in the local pub, as there were four of us, we also managed a few hands of Solo in between trips ashore. By

5 O'clock we were on the final cut, so we all stayed aboard preparing everything for boxing up the next day, and were finished by 7:30 and on our way home by 7:45, and being paid until 11pm. The next morning we cleaned everything up and checked the oil feed to the cylinder, then boxed it all up ready for engine trials that afternoon. We returned from the pub after a quick pint and after making sure that the engine turned nice and freely, we disengaged the turning gear and I went to fetch the Chief Engineer. He soon appeared with the Second Engineer, and they prepared the engine for starting while we hoisted all our gear up on deck, ready to go ashore. It wasn't long before the engine was turning over and the chief was satisfied that everything was running well, so we boarded the launch about 4pm and set off for home.

I have mentioned the 'Link One' in some detail, because coincidentally, the last ship that I worked on while with the Graving Dock was her sister ship the 'Link Two,' more of which I shall mention later.

Chapter Twelve

Hell Ship

We often worked on ships belonging to little known companies such as the Black Star Line of Ghana. The first ship that they owned the 'Volta River' could only be described as a hell ship, it was an old Sam Boat built during the war, but unlike the ones owned by Harrisons it was in an appalling condition. The company did progress rapidly, eventually having something like sixteen vessels under their name by the mid 1960s; all their ships were named after African rivers. We boarded the 'Volta River' on a cold morning a few days before Xmas, looking forward to a warm up once we entered the engine room. She had just docked that morning and was berthed on the South Quay in the West India Dock. After going up the gangway we noticed a bit of a commotion going on by one of the holds, the docker's had just removed the hatch covers and were throwing lengths of timber down into the hold. We went up and had a look to see what it was all about, the hold was loaded with hardwood from the African forests, but at first glance it all seemed to be on the move, the whole interior was infested with black rats, some of them were of unbelievable size. Obviously none of the docker's were prepared to handle any of the cargo, so the hatch covers were replaced so that the holds could be gassed. We entered the accommodation, looking for the engine room entrance, to be confronted by absolute filth and squalor, we went down the alleyway which was infested with cockroaches that made no attempt to run for cover as they usually did on other ships, as we made our way towards the engine room door they were making a crunching noise as we stepped on them. I remember looking into what must have been the crew's mess room, it was just a bare metal box, there was no furniture of any sort and the floor was bare metal. Squatting around the perimeter were several crew members eating what must have been their dinner.

Although they were squatting down I could see they were very tall, their skin was the colour of ebony and their hair seemed to climb above their heads in a frenzy of jet black tiny curls. The only clothes they had on was some sort of drab coloured sarong like garment, as I looked I noticed a cockroach slowly making its way across the bare foot of the man nearest the door. They were eating their food with their fingers, from tin plates which were placed in front of them on the bare metal floor. As we walked past they all looked up with a sad dejected expression, that made me think of the slave ships that I had read about at school.

Dick opened the door to the engine room and we were knocked back by the intense heat that rushed out at us.

"Bloody hell, I don't fancy working down there," said Peter.

We didn't really have much choice, the job had been taken on by the Graving Dock, and we were there to do it, Peter said there might be a chance to negotiate some 'heat money' so we had better get below and see what had to be done. By the time we reached the cylinder tops we were running in sweat, the hand rails were much too hot to hold, so we had to wrap rag around our hands before going down the ladders. By the time we reached the control platform at the bottom of the engine room it was slightly cooler. We were greeted by the chargehand and Tommy Wright who was one of the other fitters, he was accompanied by Sid who had recently left the fitting shop to join him outside. He had been put with Tom, and in fact remained with him for the rest of his time. The main job was to remove the Low Pressure [L.P.] cylinder cover and make and fit a new joint. The cover was about six feet in diameter and was held down by a circle of large nuts, measuring about five inches across the flats. This meant that we would be working on the cylinder tops, the hottest place in the engine room. Working in pairs we took turns in removing the nuts, which had to be done with a heavy driving spanner and a 28 pound hammer, the heat was so bad that it was only possible to remove one or perhaps two nuts in one go. This was mainly because it was too hot to stand on the cylinder cover for more than five minutes, before the heat came through the soles of your boots. The nuts were eventually removed and the heavy gang chained blocked the cover up and swung it clear. As it was now tea time, and no one fancied the ships tea, we decided to go down the quay to Aunty Kate's, it was nice to get out on deck for some fresh air, but by the time we reached the secret panel in the railings alongside Kate's, we were chilled to the bone from the East wind blowing from the river, up through the locks.

The Volta River was by far the worst ship that I ever worked on, what it must have been like to have gone to sea on I couldn't imagine, the Chief Engineer was a Greek, the rest of the engineers and what deck officers I saw were made up from all nationalities and how they communicated with each other was a mystery. We returned to the ship from Kate's, determined to get the job done by the end of the week so that we wouldn't miss our Xmas Eve lunch time hydraulic session in 'The Gun' which was only five minutes walk from the ship. Our plans were nearly thwarted by the surveyor, who came aboard the next morning and after carrying out

The Gun where Lord Nelson is reputed to have had assignations with Lady Hamilton. It was the writers 'local' during his apprenticeship days and is still much the same today as it was in the 1950s.

his inspection demanded that a lot of extra work needed to be carried out. There was no hope of completing all the repairs before Xmas, but as some of the men were prepared to work over the Xmas period, it took the pressure off us, this enabled us to slip away at about mid day on Xmas Eve to The Gun.

The inside of The Gun was quite small by comparison with most of the other pubs in the area, so it soon became packed solid with local dock workers, this included the women from the P.L.A. canteen, which was just inside the West India Dock, so it wasn't long before a good old knees up was in progress and a good time was had by all. Luckily ships like the Volta River were the exception rather than the rule.

Chapter Thirteen

The Union

In complete contrast were the four big sisters of the Ellerman fleet, these were the 'City of York,' 'City of Durban,' 'City of Exeter,' and the 'City of Port Elizabeth'. These were all built between 1952 and 1954 and were 13345 tons gross, the 'City of Port Elizabeth' was slightly more at 13363 tons gross. They were all powered by twin, six cylinder Doxford diesels which gave them a speed of just over 16 knots.

Externally it was difficult to tell them apart, the interior decor being the main difference, although they were large ships, they only carried 100 first class passengers plus general cargo. These four vessels were considered by many to be the finest looking ships to use the London Docks during the 1950s and 60s, they operated a monthly service to South and East Africa, returning via the continent to London's Royal Albert Dock, where they berthed opposite the central station halfway down the North quay. It was from here that most

Ellerman Lines 1952 City of Port Elizabeth (13363 tons gross). One of four sisters worked on by the writer while in London's Royal Albert Dock. She was powered by two 6 cylinder Doxford diesels.

of their passengers came aboard, many of these would be government officials and leading business men and their wives. Our usual work on these fine ship's was to open up the main engines for their regular surveys, this would include the stripping out of bottom end and eccentric bearings, removing pistons and changing rings, and checking and adjusting bearing clearances.

These jobs would all be done by the ships own engineers while away from the U.K. but when they were in the London Docks they were not allowed to do any repairs, the only things they could do was in connection with the general running of the ships systems, such as transferring fuel and pumping bilges and looking after the generators. The reason

Aerial view of London's Royal group of docks looking West. The King George V Dock is in the foreground. The large dry dock can be seen at the far end. The Royal Albert Dock is on the right, with the Royal Victoria Dock in the distance. At the top end of the Royal Albert Dock just below the bridge, the white ship berthed at a slight angle is a banana boat unloading her cargo at the special banana berth facility. (Museum in Docklands).

for this was the unions, they had an immense stranglehold on the way things were done in the docks, if you fell foul of the unions it could cost you your job. I had already witnessed the ten week strike, all that it seemed to me to have achieved was the loss of a great deal of work, the increase in basic pay gained would take years to recuperate. I never saw any productive benefit from the activities of the unions, their methods certainly cost the ship owners a lot of money, and led to a lot of work being diverted to the Continent which should have been done in the U.K. Their restrictive practices rule was a classic example of shooting themselves in the foot, from having a blinkered dictatorial outlook.

A memorable example of this, was when one morning we had to go down to the King George V. Dock at Woolwich to repair a window on the 'Gothic,' launched in 1948 she was one of Shaw Savill's largest ships at 15911 tons gross. She was used for the Royal tour of Australia and New Zealand in 1953.

The window was in one of the 1st class cabins, she normally carried 85 first class passengers. To repair the window in accordance with union rules, it took twelve men to do a

Shaw Savill Lines 15911 tons gross,twin screw Gothic. Seen here discharging in London's King George V Dock. Launched in 1948, and one of many of that Line's vessels that the writer worked on in the 1950s.
She was used for the Royal Tour of Australia and New Zealand in 1953. She was scrapped, following a severe fire while homeward bound from New Zealand in 1969.

job that could have easily have been done by two men. this ridiculous situation required one fitter and his mate plus their apprentice, which was myself, one plumber and his mate with their apprentice, one electrician and his mate, one shipwright and his mate and one boilermaker and his mate, making it twelve in all.

Our part in the job was to disconnect the chain from the winding mechanism, then to reconnect it after the plumbers had fitted a new glass in the frame. The electricians had to remove some wiring from behind the plywood panelling that the shipwrights had removed and the boilermakers had to dismantle a piece of metal framework from around the window frame. We were on board for four hours, to do a job that took us a total of ten minutes to do, it did however give me plenty of time to look over the ship, especially the engine room.

Towards the end of my apprenticeship I had reason to attend a union meeting at a pub in Limehouse. Slim our shop steward, who always looked after the interests of the apprentices told me that I had been paying too much in union dues, it was something to do with the month in which I was born, apparently it just put me in a different year as far as union fees were concerned, to reclaim the over payment I would have to take it up at the next union meeting.

I arrived at the pub, to find it full of union members having a good drink in the bar downstairs, after making enquiries I was told that the actual meeting was taking place upstairs. I went up and found the large room where it was being held, and on entering I was suprised to see no more than a dozen people sitting there. They were listening to a rat faced man who was sitting behind a long table on a raised platform, he was flanked on each side with several other union officials. The rat faced person was going on about raising money for the cause, and as I entered he pointed to one of the many empty chairs, indicating for me to take a seat. I had to sit through his ramblings for about half an hour, after which they held some sort of vote, where most of the people present held up their hands to say they were in favour, he then asked if there were any questions.

This was obviously my chance to put my point forward, I stood up and he asked me my name, I was then welcomed as brother Carpenter and asked what I had to say. I explained that I had been paying too much in dues and felt that I was entitled to a rebate of £7:50, this was a week and a half's basic wages at the time. They denied it was possible to pay more than the correct amount, and under no circumstances would they be prepared to reimburse me any money. I argued with the rat faced person, who insisted on calling me brother, I told him I wasn't his brother and as far as I was concerned he could keep his union, he then threatened me with disciplinary action and if I did not comply with his directives, he would see to it that I never worked in the docks again. His attitude showed me what the union was really like, and I wanted no part of it, as it happened my apprenticeship was nearing completion and as I was going to sea, his threats never worried me. I think the problem was of the ordinary working mans making, although they said they attended the union meetings, very few actually went into the meeting, preferring a pint of beer in the bar downstairs to listening to the rat faced person ranting on in an effort to increase his power within the union. The few regulars that attended the meetings, voted each other into office and gained full control, I realised that this was how a minority group could gain control over the majority. There have been cases right through history where this has happened, the Nazi party in the 1930s was a classic example, and the one that is occurring at the present time under the guise of the so called common market, where the very core of the British way of life is under severe threat.

Sometimes when working on a ship, we might have a union orientated person on the same job. They would make it their business to go round every morning looking for freshly painted nuts and bolts, or nuts that had cracked or disturbed paint around them, indicating that the ships engineers had been working during the night on a repair to the relevant component. If any evidence of this was found it would result in everyone being called off the ship until some sort of agreement was reached.

There occurred an amusing incident with a Greek tramp ship which was moored alongside the yard in the Blackwall Basin. Over the course of a weekend the ships engineers carried out some major repairs to the main engine, this required the turning of the engine with the turning gear. The turning gear was a large electric motor, driving a gear which was engaged with a gear ring on the flywheel, as most ships didn't have gear boxes, once the turning gear was started it would also turn the propeller.

The Greek ship had no cargo, so it rode high with at least one propeller blade out of the water, unfortunately the crew failed to check the stern of the vessel to make sure that it was clear of any obstructions. Unknown to them a fully laden barge had drifted under the stern, so that when they started the turning gear the propeller came round and cut a great hole in the barge which sank ruining its cargo. The propeller blades were so badly damaged that the ship had to be put in the dry-dock to have a new propeller fitted. I can't begin to imagine who paid for what, the insurance company probably used the fact that the crew shouldn't

A period advert for RYE-ARC Ltd.
Their yard was at Ovex Wharf, just to the South of the locks to The West India Docks.
The yard closed around 1960. The apprentices were amalgamated into other firms on the river.

have been doing the work as a get out clause.

My own opinion, especially as time went on and I found out more about how things were done, was that the restrictive practices as laid down by the unions were counter productive, instead of securing future employment for its members, it had the adverse effect of seeing a lot of ships going to the continent to have major repairs carried out. The rot set in during the late 1950s, an example of this was the closure of the ship repair firm of Rye-Arc, which was situated just the other side of the main entrance to the West India Docks at Ovex Wharf just off Manchester Road. They were one of the main ship repair firms on the river and had two dry-docks. I knew some of their apprentices as they attended Poplar Technical College at the same time as myself and they were extremely worried about their future. Luckily they were integrated into the remaining firms and their indentures were transferred so that they could complete their apprenticeships.

While at college I made friends with many apprentices from most of the ship repair firms

Advertisement for Blundell & Crompton Ltd. One of the oldest ship repair firms on the river, and one of the last to cease trading. The ship in the picture, seen here in The Royal Albert Dock's dry dock is the 6017 tons gross Clan Maclean (1947), one of Clan Lines fleet of over thirty ships which traded world-wide.

129

in the area, such as Badger's who were at Millwall dry-dock, and Blundell & Compton, who's works were in the West India Dock Road, I often had to go there when I worked in the fitting shop. This was to collect copper pipework that they made on behalf of the Graving Dock. They had their own Copper-smiths department and could manufacture copper components to a standard second to none. I always enjoyed my errands to their premises, as it meant a walk right up the North Quay past all the sugar warehouse's with the heavy aroma of molass'es permeateing from their dark forbidding interiors. The last, No.1 just inside the dock gate has been sympatheticlly restored and is now the site of the Museum in Docklands. A visit is a definate must for anyone interested in the history of the docks and in particular Victorian architecture.

The other place that I was sometimes sent to in the same area was the premises of the shipchandlers Davey's, they were at the far end of West India Dock Road opposite the Queen's Hotel in Limehouse. Davey's was truly an Aladins cave, a wonderful smell of hemp and tar enveloped you as you entered through the door and the place was crammed full of every conceivable item of a nautical nature.

Then there were the apprentices from Harland & Wolff at

Port Lines 1947 twin screw Port Pirie (10561) tons gross.
One of many Port Line ships worked on by the writer during his Apprenticeship.

130

North Woolwich, R.H. Green & Silley Weir at Blackwall and Royal Mail Lines from the Victoria Dock. Later when I went to sea I always made a point of visiting other company's ships that might be berthed nearby, on the off chance that I might know one of their engineers from our apprenticeship days. I rarely had any luck with these visits, but I was always made welcome, as it made a change to talk to somebody from another ship and exchange gossip over a few beers.

Advertisement for R.H. Green & Silley Weir Ltd.
Their main yard was at Blackwall adjacent to the Orchard Dry Dock. The picture shows P & O's 9080 tons gross Soudan (1948) discharging at the dolphins at the South East end of King George V Dock.

Chapter Fourteen

Real Curry

One of the reasons that we looked forward to working on Ellerman ships were their curries. They carried a Lascar crew, with British officers so that curry was always on the menu. During the 1950s it was very hard to find an Indian Restaurant, there were plenty of Chinese ones, especially in the China Town area of Limehouse, such as 'The East & West,' where if you ordered a chicken curry it was more likely you would be eating pigeon rather than chicken. Just up the road from there was 'Hell's Kitchen' which was run by a gigantic Negro who specialised in curries with the hottest spices known to civilisation.

None of these could compare with the curries that could be had on the Ellerman ships, or 'City Boats' as they were called. At lunch time a visit to the galley, and for the cost of a shilling [5p] a plate of curry and rice could be had, the quality of which could not be equalled in any shore based establishment. The other thing that we always looked forward to was the coffee, which must have been brewed in some mysterious way, and was always delicious, coming a close second to the coffee on the Scandinavian ships that we worked on across the river in the Surrey Docks, where reindeer steaks were the order of the day.

The favourite 'City Boats' were the four sisters already mentioned, the 'York' the 'Exeter' the 'Durban' and the 'Port Elizabeth,' we made a point of keeping in with the Lascar galley staff, especially the cook or "Bhandary" as he was known as, we always called them chef, a title that they revelled in.

It was customary to have our morning coffee break on a landing, halfway down a stairway just off the galley. This stairway went down to the landing, then went down again, but in the opposite direction, to gain access to the stairway we had to go through the galley which was quite large.

Chapter Fifteen

Hawser

One morning we were sitting on the stairs, together with the heavy gang enjoying our coffee when we were joined by George Lilly the burner, and a couple of boiler makers, they were doing some plate work down in one of the holds. George was always good company and invariably came out with a far fetched yarn that had everyone in fits of laughter, one of his favourite subjects was his cat, a huge creature called 'Hawser' that devoured anything that was even remotely edible, and frequently attacked George. One of its favourite tricks was to jump on George's head from the top of the stairs and bite him on the neck. George used to say that he made the special leather skull cap with the flaps that came down over his shoulders to protect him from 'Hawser' and not to keep the sparks off him while cutting metal. Apparently he always wore the headgear around the house for protection, it was rumoured that he even slept with it on.

He once told us in his quick squeaky voice, how he acquired 'Hawser'.

It was in the 'Gun' tavern, just a few yards along the riverside from George's old cottage in Coldharbour, a place that in the 1950s was classed as a slum, but today would be classed as unaffordable. George shared the cottage with his sister Mary, and every Saturday evening they would go and have a pint or two of Stout in the 'Gun,' while they were in there, the skipper and mate from one of Watkin's tugs came in, and they were accompanied by a huge black cat. During the evening the cat took a fancy to Mary and refused to leave her, at throwing out time the skipper said that seeing as how the cat wouldn't leave her, she had better have the brute, adding that he would be glad to be rid of it.

When Mary asked the skipper the cat's name, he said he always called it 'Hawser,' because of how he came to be its custodian. Apparently their tug was one of a pair, assisting a battered old Panamanian registered tramp into the locks when the cat suddenly appeared on their deck. None of the crew had seen where it had come from, but one of the crew on the other tug was adamant that he had seen it run down the towing hawser from the bow of the ship to the tug.

As the cat was too wild to catch and the crew were too frightened to go anywhere near it, they left it alone to fend for itself. It eventually took a fancy to the Skipper and followed him everywhere, but always keeping its distance and never allowing anyone to stroke it. It looked like Hawser now preferred a shore going existence with Mary, and George's life was about to become one of misery. Hawser took to his new home with relish, he now had soft chairs to sleep on, obviously preferring these, especially George's arm chair to his old sleeping quarters on the boiler casing of the tug. George reckoned that it was his armchair, and the fact that there was a never ending supply of rats that infested his back garden that made Hawser set up a permanent home with them. Among one of the many unsociable habits that Hawser had, was the storing of dead rats for a rainy day. Mary would find them in all sorts of places around the cottage, George's chair being the most common.

This particular morning I remember very well, George had just sat down with his coffee and started to roll a cigarette with his special cigarette making gadget when one of the heavy gang asked him how Hawser was getting on.

"Don't talk to me about that bloody animal, I've had a hell of a night all because of him," replied George in his high pitched squeaky voice.

He then went on to tell us that he had just got into bed and was trying to get comfortable, when he felt a lump under his pillow, he lit the lamp and discovered that Hawser had stored a half eaten rat there.

"Right that's it," he shouted to himself. He stormed down the stairs, grabbed Hawser by the neck from his armchair, and overcoming his inherent fear of the beast, dragged him into the scullery. He opened the lid of the Copper, and after a struggle managed to get Hawser inside. For readers not familiar with a Copper, it was a cylindrical container, that looked a bit like a dustbin, it stood vertically on four short cast iron legs and on the top was a lid that hinged open. Near the bottom of the cylinder was a tap, operated by a lever and underneath was a gas ring. Water would be put in at the top, and heated by the gas ring below, its main use was for boiling clothes in, or as a means of getting hot water for a bath. The water would be drained off from the tap near the base into a bucket and then tipped into the bath.

After George had shut the lid, he placed a 56Ib weight that he used as a door stop on it, and then connected a hose pipe from the tap in the sink to the tap in the base of the Copper, opened up both taps, and thought, that's finally got rid of him! When the water started coming out from under the lid, he shut the taps and went to bed after throwing the half eaten rat out of the window.

It was low water at 5am so he was up by 4.45 and off down the garden, he climbed down the old iron ladder to the foreshore and dug Hawsers grave, thinking how lucky it was that the tide was out, thus enabling him to get Hawser buried before Mary was up and about, so that when she asked where the cat was, he would say that it had probably found somewhere better live.

Exhausted and covered with mud he returned to the Copper to collect Hawser, as he was telling us this, it became obvious that one or two of the heavy gang were upset, and one called him a cruel bastard. One of the Boilermakers asked George if he managed to bury Hawser before Mary found out.

"Didn't have to as it happened," answered George. "When I opened the lid he was sitting there, looking up smiling at me with his great whiskers sticking out like welding rods, and a great bloated belly spread all over the bottom of the Copper, the bastard had drunk all the water!"

There was a moments silence, when suddenly on realising that once again George had been spinning another of his yarns, everybody bombarded him with whatever came to hand, such as half eaten rolls or lumps of oily rag.

Unfortunately Hawsers fate was already sealed, as some weeks later George told us while we were having a tea break at one of the Mobiles of his final demise. It was a Saturday evening, George and Mary went off to the Gun for their usual couple of stouts, they were normally accompanied by Hawser but for some reason he wasn't around. When they came home, about 10:45 and opened the front door, George said to Mary.

"Something smells good, I didn't know you were cooking a supper."

"I'm not," replied Mary.

They went to the cast iron range, opened the oven door and there was Hawser curled up in a ball and done to a turn. They both blamed each other for shutting him in, and since the incident they hadn't spoken to each other.

As George was recovering from the bombardment by his gullible audience, some of the Lascar crew started coming down the stairs carrying boxes of full of stores on their heads on their way down to the main ships stores which were a few flights below. We had to move aside for them, and as they reached the landing and turned in the opposite direction and went down the next flight of stairs, the boxes on their heads came level to where we were sitting. It was an opportunity too good to be true, the heavy gang were able to lift out whatever was on top of the boxes without the bearer being aware. Some had boxes of spanners which were replaced in the next bearers box, it was an unwritten rule that no one ever removed tools of any description that belonged to the ship. Others had tins of peaches on the top, these were quickly hidden inside boiler suits, to be eaten later down in the engine room. One of the heavy gang, Big Joe who always spoke so quietly that it was difficult to understand what he was saying, lifted out a large cylindrical container made of some sort of cardboard with a tin lid and base. It was labelled Bombay Duck.

"I've never had an Indian duck before," whispered Joe. "I'll have the miss'is cook it for our supper tonight," he said as he prized off the lid to inspect the contents.

As soon as he removed the lid there was an awful smell of fish.

"Didn't you know that Bombay Duck was dried fish," said one of the boilermakers.

"Blimey I can't take this home, it will stink out the whole street, I'll have to get rid of it," he whispered.

It was too late to put it on one of the Lascars boxes as they had now finished loading, Joe tried the porthole but the ring nuts were seized so he couldn't get it open.

"You'll have to dump it overboard from up on deck," said Peter,

"Don't let them see it as we go out of the galley," he added.

The carton was too big to hide inside a boiler suit, so we all left together to give him some cover.

The next morning we went along to the galley for our coffee, to be told in no uncertain terms by the Serang who was head of all the Indian crew that we were very naughty men and that shore gangs were now banned from the galley, there would be no more coffee or curries in future. This was devastating news, especially as we didn't know the reason for the ban.

After further questioning the Serang pointed across to the large stainless steel soup cauldron just inside the galley by the flight of stairs where we normally had our tea break. There was a great amount of activity going on around it by the galley staff, one was holding a steam hose into the top of it and great clouds of steam were escaping from around the lid.

The Sarang then managed to explain in his mixture of pigeon English and Lascari which we were all quite familiar with, that the previous evening the Captain had been served up his vegetable soup and after one mouthful, he rushed out of the dinning saloon and was violently sick, when he returned, looking very green around the gills he announced the whole of the galley staff were to be sacked and sent back to India on the first available ship. This to them was a fate worse than death, as the status and the regular allotment from their meagre wages that they sent home each month put them very high up in the social order in the villages where they came from.

Closer inspection of the contents of the soup cauldron

by the Chief Steward, revealed the remains of a well boiled cardboard carton and two circular tin lids. It didn't take him long to put two and two together and report his findings to the old man, who then relented on sacking the galley staff, but issued a directive that in future no shore gang would be allowed into the galley of any of the Ellerman ships.

It was months before we were able to work our way back into the good books of the galley staff to enable us to get our lunch time curry which we had to take to the engine room to eat, our usual spot on the staircase remained out of bounds for the rest of my apprenticeship, as did the ship's coffee. Big Joe who admitted that he had disposed of the Bombay Duck into the soup cauldron on our way out of the galley, led a dogs life for the duration.

Chapter Sixteen

Vermin

The work that we did on the City Boats was quite varied, it ranged from boiler repairs, main engine work, engine room auxiliary plant and repairs to steam winches and steering gear. This sometimes required the removal of the steam pipes that ran alongside the deck hatches that supplied steam to the deck machinery.

These pipes were well lagged with asbestos, that over the years had become very hard so that the only way to get to the pipe flanges was to break up the asbestos, using a hammer and chisel. This would disturb the cockroaches that infested the warm area between the pipes and the hatch coamings, they would start to run out in two's and three's but once the pipe was disconnected and pulled free, they would appear in their thousands running all over the deck in a frantic effort to find new hiding places. They moved in all directions and at incredible speed, so that within seconds they all disappeared into what seemed solid platework. How they existed in such an inhospitable place is a mystery, as much of the time when the ships were at sea the decks would be awash.

One of the worst jobs on these ships was repairing pipework down aft in the Lascars quarters, just going down there was bad enough, there would be old bicycles, Singer sewing machines, these were highly valued as they would be taken back to their villages where there was a great demand for them, they had to be a Singer no other make would do. All this together with all sorts of other junk would be piled up in every companionway, roosting on top of all this would be the chickens.

They occupied every suitable perch, and often landed on your head while you were stripping out an old steam pipe, which would be encrusted with their droppings. Once the pipe was removed, millions of cockroaches would swarm over everything, it was imperative to tie string around the bottoms of your boiler suit and also round the cuffs. After finishing work we had to check all our clothes for the creatures, just in case we took any home with us, sometimes when the infestation was so bad that we couldn't work the quarters would have to be fumigated, on these occasions we would all have to leave the ship. However on our return we very rarely found a dead cockroach, and the removal of a pipe would reveal just as many as there were in the first place. It was rumoured that they had some sort of telepathic power that enabled them to leave the ship and return when it was all clear. It was certainly a fact that the chemical used for the fumigation process affected us more than it did them, the creatures are indestructible, and I am sure that one day they will inherit the Earth. One of the old boilermakers told me that he once worked for a marine salvage company, and when they raised a ship that had lain on the sea bed for seven years cockroaches appeared within hours of it surfacing, he reckoned their eggs could lay dormant for years, awaiting the right conditions to hatch.

The Ellerman group of companies probably had more ships than any other company, with the possible exception, strange as it might seem, of British Rail who had a vast amount of tonnage. One of Ellermans ships, the City of Chicago was always used by Sir John Ellerman for his trips abroad, she was launched in 1950 and was 7622 tons with a speed of 15 knots. For some reason he preferred this ship to any of the seventy odd other vessels in his fleet, it was one of the ships that we regularly worked on, and when Sir John was due to make a trip on board her, the Graving Dock had to get the ship looking perfect for his impending voyage. This would include getting rid of all the rust spots in the paintwork and varnishing all the woodwork to yachting standards. We were told that as he was wheelchair bound, the most he ever saw of the ship was when he came aboard and the small area of deck at the end of the alleyway adjacent to his cabin, so it made it seem like a bit of a pointless exercise. However it did give the Graving Dock a nice amount of work to do and helped to keep people employed.

Chapter Seventeen

The Rolls

One of the ships that I remember well was the Baron Ardrossan, one of the many Hogarth owned vessels that we worked on. She was launched in 1954 at 5254 tons and had a speed of 12 knots.

One of our jobs on her was to change some superheater tubes, these are located right up at the back end of the boiler, and for some reason this operation came within the fitters domain and not the boilermakers. To carry out this job it was necessary to crawl in through the furnace door and across the fire grate to the back end of the boiler. This often meant going in not long after the boiler had been blown down, so that it would be very hot inside. After disconnecting the offending superheater tubes, they would be manoeuvred out through the furnace door, by the time this was done and the new ones fitted we would be as black as coal. The fine carbon dust became engrained into the skin and very difficult to remove, even after a long soak and a scrub in a hot bath it only removed the surface carbon. A couple of hours later, while out for the evening especially in the warm atmosphere of a pub or dancehall you would suddenly start to turn black, the collar and the cuffs of your shirt would become so stained that no amount of scrubbing could get rid of it, so the garment would have to be thrown away. There was no doubt about it, working up the back end of a boiler ruined your social life for two to three days afterwards.

Usually it was not possible to wash anywhere after finishing work. If we were lucky, we sometimes found a bucket that we filled from the boiler drains, or a bleed off pipe from one of the water circulating pumps. There was nearly always a tub of soft soap somewhere in the engine room, so that occasionally we were able to clean up to a certain extent, but invariably had to travel home in a pretty awful state.

The reason I remember the Baron Ardrossan so well was that it changed part of my life completely. After leaving the ship I boarded the bus to take me round the Isle of Dogs to the foot tunnel by the Island Gardens to cross under the river to Greenwich. When I came to get on the bus at Greenwich Church the conductor held out his arm showing the palm of his hand with his fingers pointing upwards, and said.

"Not you mate, try the next one."

It took me a few seconds to realise what he meant, I was so dirty, probably more so than the old time chimney sweeps used to get, so I could see his point and I stepped back off the bus. I had not had any trouble with the bus over on the Island, it might have been because the conductor hadn't seen me get on, or perhaps they were more used to people being in that condition due to the close proximity of the ship repair yards. That evening I had to wait for the third bus before I was allowed on, even then it was on the condition that I stood downstairs for the duration of the journey.

It was on the way home that I decided that I wasn't prepared to put up with being treated like a second class citizen, even though I fully understood the reason for it. As my faithful old Norton was now off the road due to the new ten year test, I made up my mind that I would take my driving test and buy a Rolls Royce, the idea gave me a certain amount of satisfaction as I thought to myself that London Transport could keep their bloody buses.

In due course I passed the driving test and obtained my license and began to look around for a suitable car. The breakdown truck mechanic was quite right about the old Rolls Royce's and how it was possible to pick one up at a reasonable price. After looking at several, all of which seemed to be in good condition, but the asking price being a bit more than I was prepared to pay, I was told of one that was parked in the street in Notting Hill waiting for the breakers to collect it.

It sounded like it was just what I was looking for, so having obtained directions I set off to have a look. I found the street, and sure enough at the far end I could see what could only be a Rolls Royce, as I came nearer I could see that it must have been there for some time. The tyres were well down, one almost flat, and it was covered in a layer of road grime and dead leaves and I couldn't help noticing, even from some distance, that one of the front wings was badly damaged. I finally reached it and started to have a look round, I soon realised that it was a 'Phantom Two' with Landaulette coachwork. I peered in through one of the filthy windows and was astonished to see that the interior looked to be in immaculate condition.

As I was looking it over a man came out of a shop opposite that sold tyres, and shouted across.

"What are you up to mate."

"Do you know if its for sale," I replied.

He came across the road with his hands in the pockets of his boiler suit smoking a cigarette saying,

"Well yes and no, the breaker's yard down the road are supposed to be collecting it, they want it for the aluminium and have offered us £65 for it, if you are interested you can have it for £75, that will cover the cost of fitting battery and making sure it starts on the button. I know it runs O.K. because it was driven here after the wing got damaged," it's a 1930 Phantom Two with coachwork by Thrupp and Maberly

It all sounded too good to be true, I agreed to buy it for the £75 he was asking and left him a deposit to make sure the breakers didn't take it away.

The writers 1930 Rolls Royce Phantom Two with Landaulette coachwork by Thrupp & Maberly. Purchased in 1959 for £75.

"Come back this time next week and you will be able to drive it away," he said. Forty two years later £75 does not sound like a lot of money, but then in 1959 it represented thirteen weeks basic wages, however this was offset by the overtime and bonus that was now coming in on a regular basis, so seeing that I was only an apprentice I was quite well off.

The following week I arrived at the tyre shop, having been given a lift by a friend who had borrowed his fathers car, to find the Rolls looking quite smart, they had even washed all the leaves off and pumped up the tyres. The man started it on the button, and all was as he had promised it would be the previous week, I paid him the balance and set off for home. I put a few gallons of petrol in the tank on the way home, but by the time I arrived it was nearly empty again, I soon realised why these old Rolls Royce's were not wanted by the average car owner.

It didn't take me long to remove and repair the damaged wing, and after a good clean up the car looked immaculate inside and out. It weighed just over two and a half tons, and with an engine capacity of 7600 c.c. it was a leviathan by any standards. The first time I went to work in the Rolls it caused quite a sensation, especially among the motor orientated officianardo's. I had many amusing incidents while using the car in the docks. There was a time while working on the 'Silvio' one of the Ellerman Wilson ships, which was berthed in the Western dock of the London Dock, just below Tower Bridge at Wapping. I always found this a fascinating place to work, with its

Copy of original receipt for 1930 Rolls Royce.

magnificent warehouse stacks and fortress like walls it was a no go area to ordinary Londoners, who had no idea of the bustling activity that went on behind its enormous dirt grimed walls. Making the dock all the more mysterious were its underground vaults, which covered an area of some 22 acres. The ships that used the London Dock during the 1950s were mostly what were known as short sea traders, from companies such as, General Steam Navigation, [G.S.N.], Curries, Ellerman Wilson line, Oranje line, Hermans, and many other foreign owned ships. Some of these ships were among the best looking vessels to use the London river, often looking like smaller versions of the blue water liners that frequented the Royal Group of docks further down river at Woolwich.

The 'Silvio' was one such ship, she was launched in 1947, had a tonnage of 1798 and a steam reciprocating main engine with an exhaust turbine.

Aerial view of London Docks looking West.
St. Katharines Dock can be seen just below Tower Bridge.
Below St. Katharines Dock are the Eastern Dock on the left and the Western Dock on the right. The writer frequently worked on ships berthed on these quays.
Beneath the large warehouse stacks that divide St. Katharines Dock and the East and West docks were some 22 acres of underground vaults that were mainly used for the storage of wine. The surrounding quaysides were used for wine guaging and repairing barrels. (Museum in Docklands).

145

On this particular incident, I had parked the Rolls alongside the warehouse nearest the ship, my usual parking place and a large area around it was covered with recently unloaded barrels of port. The car was facing the main dock entrance about 100 yards away. We had been working on the 'Silvio' for three days and this was our last day.

At lunch time Peter, Dick, and I had returned from a cafe just outside the dock gate in Pennington Street, it was run by a Hungarian who served up a superb Goulash, so we made a point of going there when we were working in that area. As it was a nice sunny day we stretched out on the forward hatch to catch a bit of sun, Peter was smoking a cigarette, and when he finished I saw him flick the dog end across the deck and over the ships side. About twenty minutes later we heard shouting coming from where Peter had flicked his cigarette and the ships alarms started ringing.

"Sounds like the ships on fire," said Peter dryly.

We raised ourselves from the hatch, to find great clouds of smoke rising from over the ships side, some of the ships crew were running up with fire extinguishers and there were several people looking over the side. We strolled over to see what it was all about, and as soon as I looked over I could see what had happened, Peter's dog end had gone over the side and landed in a rolled up tarpaulin on the foredeck of a barge moored alongside. As a pair of lightermen unrolled the tarpaulin, another was emptying a fire extinguisher at it. They soon had it under control and by the time it was completely unrolled, there was a series of large smouldering holes along its length.

"I wonder how that happened," said Peter as he lit another cigarette, then added,

"Looks like its time to make ourselves scarce and get below."

We finished all our work on the 'Silvio' by about 3pm and everyone was keen to get away, unfortunately the lorry that was supposed to be there to take the lifting tackle and the heavy gang back to the yard hadn't turned up. Someone phoned the office, and were told that it had been delayed down at the Albert Dock, and due to the heavy traffic it wouldn't be here until at least 5pm, so it meant that the heavy gang would have to hang around waiting for it.

"I've got the Rolls just round the corner, why don't we all go in that, there's plenty of room for the gear on the floor in the back," I said to Archie the foreman of the heavy gang.

"Do you think we'll all get in?" he replied.

"Of course, I'll go and bring it round to the gangway," I answered.

I went off to get the car and by the time I returned they had piled all the gear up at the bottom of the gangway. Peter had his Vauxhall there so he took our tool box and gave Dick a lift down to Limehouse.

The rear compartment of the Rolls had two pull out occasional seats, so that when they were folded into the division it left something like 25 square feet of floor area. We soon piled everything in, Archie had found a couple of clean sacks which he put down to protect the carpet, there was plenty of room but I was a bit concerned about the weight of it all on the floorboards. Archie sat next to me in the front and the three other heavy gang climbed in the back and we set off, as we drove down between the warehouses towards the gate, the P.L.A. policeman on duty appeared and as we drew level with him he stood to attention and saluted in a very formal manner. I stopped the car, but before I could say anything Archie lent forward, wound down the window and said.

"Graving Dock scalers mate."

The policeman looked like he had been turned to a pillar of salt, his mouth dropped open, at the same time he slowly lowered his arm from his salute. It obviously took his brain some seconds to comprehend the situation, when it did he came over and said.

"You bastards," the 'you' part of the statement being quite long and drawn out, I could see that he wasn't a happy man and thought to myself that we were in for a serious going over, which would have meant unloading all the gear. Instead he leant with both arms resting on the bottom of the window frame and put his head through the open window and looked around the inside of the car in total amazement.

Luckily he saw the funny side of it, and went on to say that when he came on duty at 2pm he spotted the Rolls parked down by the warehouse and assumed that there must be an official visit by the dignitaries of the P.L.A. taking place. That being so, he didn't dare make himself a cup of tea or have a read of the paper in case their departure caught him unawares. That explained why we were given the official salute as we drew up at the gate.

"You lot must be doing all right, driving around in a car like this," he said.

"We're not doing too bad," replied Archie.

"The one with all the money is our apprentice, he's the one that owns the car," he added as he pointed to me.

With that everyone burst out laughing, including the policeman, who then said,

"Go on, you had better sod off before I nick the lot of you."

As we pulled out into Old Smithfield he gave us another very formal salute.

Since I had been working outside I hadn't had any encounters with Edgar Taylor, this was because I rarely visited the yard. I hadn't had the Rolls long, when we had a job in the dry-dock on one of the Trinity House pilot cutters. These were lovely looking little ships, resembling a large motor yacht, financially they were not very rewarding as there was rarely any overtime to be earned one them, so we would have to clock off with our disc's at 5pm.

One evening I was sitting in the Rolls, waiting for Fred the timekeeper to bring out the boxes, when I noticed Edgar come out of the main office door.

I watched him walk across to his car, which was a diesel powered Borgward, all the managers had these supplied as company cars. As he unlocked the drivers door he happened to look back, where upon he noticed the Rolls parked alongside the plumber's shop. Curiosity got the better of him and he came towards me obviously intent on finding out what a Rolls Royce was doing in his yard. He walked all round the car and stopped beside the driver's window just as I finished winding it down, I could tell that he was going to have one of his bouts of raving. He always gave the impression that he didn't know any of the apprentices, so I was half expecting what he was about to say.

"Who the bloody hell are you," he said.

I knew that he had recognised me, but I told him who I was hoping that it might calm him down a bit, but unfortunately it had the opposite effect.

"There's something going on in this yard that I know nothing about, I want to know how an apprentice can afford to run a car like this. I shall be having a close look at the timesheets, mark my words I'll find out where the fiddle is and who is involved," he said as he pointed his finger at me through the open window, his face becoming more flushed by the second.

By the time Edgar had finished with me, the whistle had gone, everyone had left the yard and the time keepers had retrieved their money boxes, as I put my disc in through the timekeepers window Fred said to me with a knowing grin,

"Upsetting Edgar again, I expect we'll all be in for it when he comes in tomorrow."

The next morning I told Peter of my encounter with Edgar.

"We had better curtail our refuelling operations for a while, just to be on the safe side. he replied.

This was a nuisance as our little fiddle with a supply of petrol was a big help as far as running the Rolls was concerned.

It so happened that Dicks niece worked up in the office, she told him that the office girls life was being made a misery by Edgar in his endeavours to satisfy his obsession with the time sheets. All this was on top of his normal frequent outbursts of abuse that often bought tears to the eyes of the girls.

Chapter Eighteen

The Smog

One of the fitters, Alf Hinds also ran an old car, it was a Riley Kestrel with a fabric roof and like many cars of the time it had pneumatic upholstery. Alf was a jovial sort of person with a wicked sense of humour, and he wasn't averse to pulling the odd practical joke on people. We were working on the 6609 ton motor ship Cape Ortegal, belonging to the Lyle Shipping Company and launched in 1946, when one morning Peter showed me a gadget, that in those days could be obtained from high street motor factors such as Halfords.

It was a tyre inflator, to use it you had to remove a sparking plug from the engine, then screw in what was in fact a non-return valve this was connected to a length of air hose, the other end of which was then put on the tyre valve. The engine was started and run at tick over and the tyre would inflate in about twenty seconds.

"This afternoon we'll slip over to Alf's car and connect this little lot up to his seat cushion, it should be interesting when he starts up to go home, I want to give him some of his own medicine," said Peter.

Just before the afternoon teabreak we left the ship and went round to where Alf had parked his car, it only took a few minutes to fit the inflator, but we had to make sure that the air line was well hidden under the carpet.

That evening we were all working to 7pm, but were away by 6pm, so Peter made sure we were in a good position to witness the results of our handy-work. We sat in his Vauxhall and watched as Alf came along and got in his Riley, we heard him start the engine, in no time at all he seemed to rise up and a great bulge appeared in the fabric roof above the drivers seat.

Suddenly Alf's head burst through the roof in a cloud of dust, there was a loud bang as the pneumatic seat burst and Alf dropped down almost disappearing below the bottom of the window, as now that the cushion had burst he was sitting on the frame of the seat

"Bloody hell I didn't think it would do that, we had better go and see if he is all right," said Peter.

We went over and I could hear the engine still pumping air into the remains of the cushion with a loud hissing sound. Alf was still sitting in the car and was visibly shaken, Peter leant in through the window and switched off the ignition and asked him if he was all right.

"I don't know what happened there, but it looks like someone got the better of me this time," replied Alf with a thin smile.

"Looks as if the roof's had it," said Peter.

"Oh, I'll soon fix that, its all rotten anyway," replied Alf looking up from his new seating position.

He climbed out of the car and opened the bonnet and immediately spotted the tyre inflator

"Nice one, I've always wanted one of them, I can't wait to use it on someone else," he remarked.

Peter had left the sparking plug on top of the engine, so Alf soon unscrewed the non return valve and fitted the plug,

Lyle Shipping Company's 6909 tons gross Cape Ortegal (1946). The writer worked on several of this company's ships, usually while berthed in The Greenland Dock in the Surrey Commercial Docks at Rotherhithe.
(National Maritime Museum, Greenwich).

he put the passenger seat cushion on the drivers side, started the car and drove off down the quay with the ragged edges of the hole in the roof flapping away, making a sound a bit like a machine gun. As the Riley disappeared round the corner of the warehouse, Peter sat with both hands on the top of the Vauxhall's steering wheel and said, "That could have been a bit dodgey, especially if he had got under way, I'm a bit concerned about the poor bastard he's going to play the same trick on though." The next day I had a look at the Riley, and saw that Alf had repaired the hole in the roof using a piece of material cut from an old mackintosh which he had stuck in place with rubber solution. The repair lasted well, and with the onset of Winter we had some work to do on the 'Jamaica Producer,' and once again I found that Alf was on the same job.

The 'Jamaica Producer' was a banana boat owned by Jamaica Banana Producers Steam Ship Co. Ltd. Built in 1935 she was 5464 tons and powered by one of the biggest triple expansion steam engines that I had seen that gave her a speed of 15 knots. During the war she had the distinction of shooting down a German bomber that was attacking her, and for some time afterwards she carried a small painted aircraft on her funnel in recognition of her kill. The 'Jamaica Producer' was berthed at the banana wharf at the North East corner of the Royal Albert Dock, just up from the cold stores where the ships of The New Zealand Shipping Co. discharged their frozen cargo's.

The banana wharf was a specially made facility, where the stems of banana's were unloaded by a moving conveyor, which went right over into the ship's hold from the shed, this enabled a continuous stream of banana stems to go from the ship into the shed and then into the special containers that were then transported by lorry or railway wagons. They came out of the hold in a green, unripe condition, occasionally some would be a bit too ripe, so they would be discarded in a heap outside the shed. By the end of the day there would be a considerable stock of over ripe stems dumped there, I was told that they were taken and fed to pigs. As soon as we went on board the banana boats Peter and I would go down the hold and select a stem that looked like it was on the turn and take it down the engine room and hang it in the stores, the banana's would soon begin to ripen, so all hands could help themselves whenever they fancied one, often leading to some uncomfortable situations for those that over indulged. The stems were not wrapped in polythene or put in cardboard containers as they were in later years, but were stored on slatted wooden shelves down in the ships hold. While searching for a suitable stem, we often came across lizards, and some sort of dark brown beetle that gave a very nasty bite, sometimes we also found birds nests tucked right up among the bunches.

One morning just as we emerged from the engine room to go ashore to the mobile, all hell broke loose down on the quay. Looking over the ships side we saw a group of docker's running about shouting, I could see one of them pointing to an old wooden crate. Another was gingerly approaching, holding a stoker's shovel as if it were a cricket bat about to hit a ball for six, another docker quickly ran up to the crate and gave it a shove with his foot and retreated at an even

A five cylinder Doxford Diesel engine of 3000 bhp. The majority of the engines that the author worked on during his time at The London Graving Dock were of this type. They were opposed piston two strokes and ranged from three to six cylinders. Their maximum running speed was 120 rpm. Engines of this type were used to power general cargo vessels such as the 'Cape Ortigal.'

153

faster rate, tripping himself up in the process and ending up on a small heap of over ripe bananas. Without warning, a huge spider the size of a dinner plate ran from under the crate and across the quay at incredible speed to the side of the shed where it tried to hide itself. The docker's all started shouting again, some of them throwing bananas from the waste pile at the creature. It ran along the edge of the shed then made a dash out into the open, the docker with the shovel found himself in its path and instinctively brought the shovel down with an axe like blow, slicing the spider in two and for a second or so, each half continued on its way. The gang of dockers slowly came over and stood round the remains, the one with shovel then scooped up each half in turn and threw them in the dock.

"It must have been in the stems on the waste heap over there," said Peter, and after a thoughtful pause added, "I'll tell you something else, I won't be going down the hold anymore, fancy that thing dropping on your neck as we were sorting out the bananas this morning."

That afternoon one of the London smog's closed in and

Jamaica Banana Producers 5464 tons gross Jamaica Producer (1934) heading for London's Royal Albert Dock with a full cargo of bananas.
Reproduced by kind permission of Foto Flite of Ashford, Kent.

brought visibility down to a few feet, this was followed by the sound of ships whistles and fog horns from the unfortunate vessels that were manoeuvreing in the confines of the dock or just outside on the river. These smogs were a nuisance as well as a serious health hazard, they brought the whole area to a virtual standstill for their duration. It also meant that I would probably have to walk home that night as the buses wouldn't be running. I rarely used the Rolls when working in the Royal group of docks, as it meant going out of my way through the Blackwall Tunnel or waiting in a never ending queue to cross the river on the Woolwich ferry.

It was much quicker to use the foot tunnel at Woolwich, or sometimes relive my boyhood days on the ferry as a foot passenger and indulge myself by watching the engines that had so fascinated me in my early years, but for some reason now seemed much smaller than I remembered them. That evening when we left the ship, we found that the smog had come down even worse and with the onset of darkness at about 4:pm. it brought visibility down to zero. Peter decided to leave his car on the quay, so we set off together, groping our way towards the dock gate. Suddenly we heard the sound of a car approaching from behind, the thick yellowish smog stopped us seeing anything, but we could tell by the sound of its exhaust as it went by that it was going much too fast for the prevailing conditions.

"Bloody fool," said Peter.

The words were hardly out of his mouth, when from somewhere up ahead came the sound of a loud bang, followed by the sound of breaking glass.

"I'll bet that was the stupid bastard that just went by, we had better see if we can find him," said Peter.

The visibility was almost down to zero so it was impossible to hurry, in fact it was difficult to know in which direction we were going. If it had not been for the railway line that we were following, we would have been completely disorientated. Its hard to imagine what the smogs were like during the 1950s, but it was easy to lose all sense of direction in one of the 'pea soupers' as we called them. We carried on for about five minutes, without seeing or hearing anything.

The smog's always brought the docks to a standstill, this was accompanied by an eerie silence quite out of character with the usual hustle and bustle and general background noise that was taken for granted, and went undetected until it all fell silent. There was only the occasional muffled sound of a fog horn from somewhere out on the river, coming from the odd unfortunate ship that had not yet found a safe mooring. Many vessels still did not have the luxury of radar, and with a fast running river like the Thames they could find themselves in a serious situation, which put the seamanship skills of the river pilots to the test.

I was just saying to Peter that we must have passed the place where the bang had come from, when we heard a car engine start up, followed by a lot of reving up and the sound of glass being run over together with a tearing noise of fabric and wood. It seemed to be quite close, but the smog played tricks on the way sound travelled. Suddenly it all went quiet, we stood straining our ears for the slightest clue as to where the incident was taking place, when we heard someone shout,

"You bastard."

This was followed by the engine being started again and the car being driven off, with the sound of the exhaust quickly being absorbed by the smog as it drew away. We continued to search the area as best we could, but found nothing to give us a clue as to what had happened, we had lost contact with the railway track that we had been following, but came upon another track that was flush with the surface so we knew that we were on the road between the sheds. Suddenly the vague shape of a railway wagon manifested itself out of the smog so we fumbled our way along it and found that it was coupled to another one, from underfoot came the sound and feel of broken glass.

"I bet this is what that car crashed into, the wagons seem to be half across the road, look there's a big piece of fabric and a lump of wood hanging on this wagon," said Peter.

I then replied that I thought we were wasting our time trying to get home, to which he agreed and suggested that we get back to the ship and wait to see if the smog lifts, if not we could always bed down in the engine room for the night. It took us a good twenty minutes to find our way back to the 'Jamaica Producer,' where we went straight down the engine room for a warm up. Here we found that most of the Graving Dock gang who were working on the ship had the same idea.

It didn't take long for a couple of card schools to get underway which soon passed the time. we also managed to scrounge a pot of tea from the cook, so any thoughts of trying to get home through the smog soon disappeared. Just before 10:30 the ships duty engineer came down for his regular engine room check and reported that a wind had sprung up and the visibility was improving by the minute. Peter and I set off to see if we could get a bus, and as we passed the spot where the railway wagons were parked, which was less than 100yds from the ship, we could see that a car had gone right under the side of one of them, leaving debris all over the place. We reached the dock entrance, to find the buses running so we were soon on our way round Silvertown to the ferry. I eventually arrived home just before midnight. The next day was our last on the 'Jamaica Producer,' she was due to sail that evening for the West Indies. We had been checking and adjusting the bottom end and eccentric bearings on the main engine, these were very large and heavy components that had to be manoeuvred with the aid of chain blocks. The bearings were cleaned up with an engineer's scraper and the correct clearance was obtained using lead wire, which was placed around the bottom half of the bearing using grease to keep it in situ. The bearing was boxed up and let down again, the lead wire was then measured with a micrometer and the appropriate amount of shims would be added or subtracted to give the correct clearance.

I arrived on the ship about 8am, it was still a bit foggy, but compared to the previous evenings 'pea souper' the visibility was quite good, I could see halfway down the Albert Dock, just making out the funnel of a City Boat berthed opposite the Central Hotel. We always patronised the Central when working in the area, as they served up a very good dinner in the bar at a fair price. I was about to go below when I heard a car coming down the quay which had a very sporty exhaust note. Out of curiosity I went to the ships rail to have a look, it was held up behind a lorry so I couldn't actually see it until it suddenly swung out and sped past the ship at an alarming rate. It was a Riley open sports car of some sort, that looked vaguely familiar. Having skidded to a halt alongside the banana shed, the driver, who was dressed in what can only be described as period attire, complete with goggles, cloth cap worn the wrong way round, and a white silk scarf which had been billowing out behind him as he drove up the quay, stepped over the side of the car without opening the door and came towards the ship.

It wasn't until he was almost at the top of the gangway, did I recognise him, it was Alf Hinds, he must have exchanged his old saloon for a sports car I remembered thinking to myself.

"Good morning Davey boy, what do think of the new car?" he said as he lifted the goggles from his face to his forehead, using both hands which were encased in a pair of leather gauntlets. He said no more, but went straight down to the engine room. After he had gone I went down to have a look at his new acquisition, I was still some yards away when I saw that it was in fact his same old Riley, no wonder it had looked familiar as it went by I thought to myself. I then realised what must have happened the night before, it was obviously Alf who had driven under the goods wagon, ripping off half the roof and breaking most of the windows in the process. How he had escaped injury was a miracle. At tea break that morning he told us all about it, after he had crashed into the wagon he managed to reverse the car out and set off home, how he ever found his way was a mystery, on the way he lost the remaining half of his roof. The smog had cleared by the time he arrived home, so he was able to have a good look at the damage. He decided the easiest way to deal with it was to saw the remaining bits of the roof down level to the tops of the doors and make an open tourer of it, so he spent several hours sawing and generally tidying up the edges to make it look presentable. He then rammed a metal rod up the exhaust pipe to break up the baffles, so as to get a nice sporty sound.

He kept the car for several months after his run in with the railway goods wagon, eventually selling it for a good profit to a Riley enthusiast who convinced himself that it was a rare sports prototype, that must have been prepared by Riley themselves for a special event, such as the Monte Carlo Rally, Alf of course saw no reason to dissolution him.

Chapter Nineteen

Millwall

Millwall Dock was one of our regular working areas. The Strick Line ships were regular visitors to these docks and were instantly recognisable by the red and blue painted chevrons on their funnels. They were always referred to as Stan Boats, as the suffix of their names always ended in 'stan' for example 'Tabaristan'. One of the more unusual jobs that we had to do was to remove all the pulley wheels from the grain elevators at McDougall's flour mill, which was known locally as the Organ pipes, due to the cylindrical shapes of the building. The flour mill could be called the modern equivalent of the windmills that once followed the line of the river around the South Eastern part of the Isle of Dogs, which gave it the name of Millwall.

I had worked on ships at the mill on many occasions but had never given the elevators any thought. It wasn't until we had to remove the pulley wheels and sheave blocks, and replace them after they had been rebushed in the fitting shop, that I realised how large the elevators were.

To get to the top pulleys we had to crawl up the grain trunking, which was the home of thousands of small white moths, as we went up we disturbed them from their resting places, turning the confined area into a white seething mass. They penetrated right into our boiler suits and became entangled in our hair, how the creatures were separated from the flour I have no idea. On the other hand, perhaps they never were. The top most pulleys were some ninety feet above the water, and ranged in size from 12 inches to 30 inches in diameter, so it was a tricky operation to remove the pin and lower the pulleys down. It was a hot day and by the time we had removed all the pulleys we were completely covered in white grain dust, which caked into a solid crust in our hair. Because our hands became covered in grease it also stuck to them in a thick layer, making them appear twice the size. We were all pleased to see the end of the job, especially as there was no bonus involved.

The other place where we often found ourselves was down in the dry-dock at Millwall. This dock was 547 feet long as opposed to the London Graving Docks dry-dock which was 450 feet long, the use of the dry-dock at Millwall enabled the Graving Dock to tender for work on slightly larger ships trading to and from the Isle of Dogs. Work on still larger vessels was undertaken in the dry-dock at the Western end of the King George V Dock down river at Woolwich which was 750 feet in length.

While working at Millwall on the 9221 ton 'Weybridge' one of Watts Watts & Company's ships, a film crew appeared one morning and started erecting name boards and placing large American cars around the area to give the impression that it was somewhere in the USA. They were using the ship repair firm of Badgers, which was adjacent to the dry-dock as their set. I had seen several films being shot in the docks, and we always took advantage of their mobile catering facilities when the opportunity arose.

Peter soon showed me the technique of impersonating a film extra, where by we were able partake of the very good meals from their mobile canteen free of charge. We were also able to find out what the film was all about and sometimes saw some of the well known stars of the fifties. The film they were shooting at the time was called 'Interpol' and starred Victor Mature. The blacksmith's and boilermaker's shops at Badgers were used for the final gunfight scenes, but when I eventually saw the film I had difficulty in recognising the places that I knew so well, which was no doubt due to the film makers skill.

The 'Weybridge' was typical of the ships owned by Watts Watts & Co., she was delivered in 1958 so she was one of the most up to date ships in service, and quite revolutionary in her design, both above and below the water line. The welfare of the crew was paramount and the companies policy was that every crew member had their own cabin. All the officers cabins came out on to a covered promenade deck which ran down the side of the ship.

As I neared the end of my apprenticeship, I started to seriously think about which shipping company I would like to go to sea with and Watts Watts came high on the list, mainly due to the excellent conditions afforded to the crew, but also like Hogarths Baron Boats they were a tramping company, so were not tied to regular routes, this would mean that I would be able to see more of the world. During the 1950s and early 60s the Merchant Navy was the only way to see all those places with strange sounding names that had intrigued me when I first saw them on the sterns of the ships on my first visit to the docks all those years before.

A 1960s Advertisement for W. Badger Ltd.
Their workshops were situated on the East side of Millwall dry dock.
The ship in the lower picture is Harrison Line's 6533 tons gross 'Factor' (1948). This was one of the many Harrison ships worked on by the writer as an apprentice.

Before the Isle of Dogs became commercialised, it was said to have some of the best agricultural land in the country. At first glance the West India and Millwall Docks with their warehouses, sheds and associated infrastructure would seem to have obliterated all the useful open land, in fact there were areas tucked away that seemed to be just as they might have been before the docks were constructed. One particular spot between the South Dock and Millwall Dock produced the finest horse radish you could find anywhere. When I found myself working nearby, I would borrow a crowbar from the ship and spend most of my lunch hour digging up a good sack full, it was hard work as the roots went down a long way, never the less it was worth it, as I used to sell most of it to a greengrocer who had a costermonger's stall in Beresford Square, Woolwich. He told me that he had regular customers for it, who tried their utmost to find out where it came from. It was so hot that if it caught you unawares it felt like your eyes were being drawn down into your nose.

I found the whole of the Isle of Dogs a fascinating place to work, as it was full of marine history. I regularly passed the wharf where the Great Eastern was built, which was on the site of Napiers old yard and the adjacent yard of the ship builders Ditchburn and Mare, and was marked by a plaque on the wall. It has been written that the Great Eastern was an unlucky and ill fated ship, but she did sterling service

Watts, Watts & Company's 9221 gross ton, 'Weybridge' (1958).
The highly individualistic design of the London firm of Watts, Watts & Co. Ltd. ships made them very popular with crews. Their accommodation provided a cabin for each crew member to the highest standards.
The Weybridge is seen here heading for London's West India Docks, powered by her 6700 bhp six cylinder Doxford Diesel engine.
Photograph reproduced by kind permission of Foto Flite, Ashford, Kent.

as a cable layer and was a credit to that great engineer Isambard Kingdom Brunel and the golden age of Victorian engineering when Great Britain led the world in heavy engineering.

The Island also had several very good pubs, the Waterman's Arms probably being the best known, bought by Daniel Farsons the well known T.V. presenter of the late 1950s, he turned it into an old time music hall establishment which became very well known as the place to go. One of the best kept secrets was The Gun, a superb example of a Thames side pub with its small terrace overlooking the river, from which you had a good view of ships inward and outward bound to the Surrey and the London Docks and the Pool of London further upstream. Owing to The Gun's adjacent position to the entrance to the West India and Millwall Docks its terrace also gave a grandstand view of the vessels using these docks. It was reputed that one of the upstairs rooms was used by Lady Hamilton for her assignations with Lord Nelson. On a

A ten cylinder double acting 12000 bhp two stroke diesel engine built by Harland and Wolff to Burmeister and Wain patent. This type of engine was used to power many of the large passenger cargo liners that the author worked on during his apprenticeship.

recent visit I was surprised and very pleased to find that it had hardly changed since the 1950s, the only noticeable difference being the removal of an interior wall to make the bar area larger. It is still possible to enjoy a beer out on the terrace, but sadly all the ships have gone and only exist in the memory of all those that lived or worked on the island and took it all for granted, never imagining for a moment that those magnificent vessels, together with a whole way of life were soon to disappear for ever.

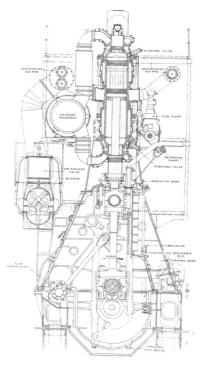

▲ A section of one of the units (cylinders) of a Burmeister & Wain double acting two stroke diesel engine. This is an example of an early model where the exhaust pistons are operated from an auxiliary crankshaft, in later models they were driven from eccentrics on the main crankshaft.

◄ Working in the crankcase of a 7500 bhp double acting two stroke Burmeister & Wain diesel engine. A rope tackle is being used to lift the large flogging spanner, being held by the writer, on to the nut at the base of the Piston rod. The circular object at the top of the picture is a light cluster.

Chapter Twenty

Rum & Rose's

The Surrey Docks at Rotherhithe was another place where I often found myself working. There was a slight advantage in working there as it meant that I didn't have to cross the river; with all its attendant problems of traffic congestion. It was still pretty bad on the South side, but by using the back doubles I was able to miss most of the hold ups.

The Surrey Docks covered a vast area, and it usually required a lot of leg work to get to the ship that we were working on. The majority of ships using these docks were timber carriers, mostly from the Baltic. They often arrived with a severe list, due to their deck cargo of timber having shifted after encountering heavy weather while crossing the North Sea. The Prince Line were also regular users with vessels such as the 3271 ton Black Prince and the 3364 ton Egyptian Prince, these used the Greenland Dock.

This dock got its name from the whaling fleet that used it during the second half of the eighteenth century, it was originally constructed in 1696 and was known as The Howland Great Wet Dock. It was the second enclosed basin to be built with direct access to the Thames and had an area of about ten acres with an entrance lock 150 feet long and 44 feet wide, adjacent to the entrance were two dry-docks and a slipway, the boundary was lined with trees to give some shelter to the vessels using the dock. It was known locally Dead Mans Dock, this was due to the vast amount of human bones that were unearthed during its construction, as it was the site of one of the many mass graves where victims of the plague or black death were disposed of. After the whaling industry declined the Greenland dock was absorbed into the vast area known as the Surrey Commercial Docks with a water area of just over 147 acres and a lineal quayage of just over five and a half miles.

One of the things that we enjoyed about working in the

Surrey Docks were our lunch time sessions in 'Rose's'. This was a small cafe on the opposite side of the road to the docks just along from Surrey Docks underground station. It was run by Rose herself, a wonderful old lady, who at that time, i.e. the late fifties, must have been in her seventies. It was a unique place and would have no chance of surviving with the attitudes of modern social standards of today. From the outside it was just like any other cafe to be found around the dock's, grime stained, peeling paintwork, and windows that were very hard to see through from the outside. If you took the trouble to look up to the roof, it was still possible to see signs of the severe damage the whole row of buildings had received during the war.

Rose was never seen in the dining area at all, she always stayed down in the kitchen at the back, reached by a short

Aerial view of the Surrey Commercial Docks, circa 1960 looking North.
In the centre foreground lies Greenland Dock. This dock was originally known as The Howland Great Wet Dock, and was the second manmade enclosed dock on the Thames, the first was at Blackwall (circa 1661).
The Blackwall Dock was used for the repair of vessels, whereas The Howland Dock was intended for the discharging of cargo in a secure environment. It was later used by the large whaling fleet and became known as The Greenland Dock.
Rotherhithe tunnel runs under the river at the top left of the picture.
(Museum in Docklands).

flight of steps. From here she served up the dinners from her array of saucepans on the cooking range that were then passed up to her customers at the top of the stairs. Quite often she was accompanied by the local 'Bobby,' who sat with her and had his dinner down in the kitchen. The usual card schools prevailed, but if all the tables were full and someone wanted to sit down with their dinner Rose would send the policeman up to clear a space, if he wasn't there for some reason or other, she would shout up to everyone to make room for her latest customer. Her orders were always obeyed instantly. Before a table was vacated, one of its occupants returned the dirty plates to the kitchen while another gave the table top a wipe over with a damp cloth that Rose made available. When it came time to pay the bill, you had to put your money in a box at the top of the kitchen stairs, then shout down to Rose how much you were putting in, and how much change if required you were taking out. The area around Rotherhithe, as with all dock areas in the fifties was populated in general by hard working, honest people who looked after their own, and I never heard of any occasion where anyone took advantage of Rose's hospitality and left without paying for their dinner. I would imagine the consequences of doing so would have been most unpleasant had they been noticed by any of her regulars.

During the last year of my apprenticeship I decided to sell the Rolls and buy a smaller model which would be more economical to run, this was mainly due to the loss of our 'subsidised' petrol supply, caused by the ever watchful Edgar Taylor, keeping a more than usual eye on the activities of the apprentices. Just before I part exchanged the Phantom Two for a Rolls-Royce 20/25 I left it parked between the sheds on Canary Wharf while working on one of the 'City Boats'. When I came ashore that evening I found that I was completely boxed in by dozens of export Rover motor cars, I suspect the local dockers took great delight in doing it.

"Looks like you will have to leave the old girl there for the night," said Peter trying to quell his amusement.

"Never mind I'll give you a lift through the tunnel as far as

Charlton," he added.

While he was talking I was quickly assessing the situation, I knew the dockers very rarely applied the hand brakes on the cars waiting shipment, so there was a chance that I might be able to shunt the row of cars in front of me, far enough forward to enable me to squeeze through a gap in the next row that I could see about thirty yards down the line.

"No I reckon I can get out," I replied to Peter.

"You'll need a tank to get out of there," he answered.

"With over seven and a half litres under the bonnet I've practically got one," I said, as I climbed into the Rolls and slowly edged up to the car in front. With no effort at all it slowly moved on to the next in line, which also moved easily. After I had taken up the slack between all the Rovers in front of me I soon had all the row of cars moving nicely. There was just enough room for them to move forward, before they reached the next shed to enable me to reach the gap where I hoped to squeeze through. The system worked well, and I was soon out into the open and on my way home, proving the old saying that there is no substitute for litres.

I decided the best thing to do for the next couple of days, as far as the Rolls was concerned was to keep a low profile, so I left it at home until we finished the job on the 'City Boat' at Canary Wharf, just in case the dockers took their revenge and blocked me in on a more permanent basis.

Soon after this incident I part exchanged the Phantom Two for a 1932 Rolls-Royce 20/25 which was a much more practical every day car, giving me on average 18mpg as opposed to the Phantoms 8mpg. I was sorry to see the old girl go, as it never gave me any trouble during the year I was its custodian, it also passed the 10 year test with flying colours.

Shortly after I acquired the 20/25, Sid announced that he was getting married and asked me if I would drive his future wife to the church on the big day and then take them up to Victoria Station the next morning.

I was pleased to be able to use the car for such an event, so I readily accepted the invitation. The wedding was in Manor Park, Essex, and it all went off very well, after the reception, we all went back to Sid's parents house in Dagenham. The time between then and the Monday morning when I awoke to go to work, has remained one of the blank periods in my life. I looked out of my bedroom window and saw the Rolls parked in its usual spot in the road outside, but I had no recollection of how it had arrived there. This was probably the only morning that I didn't look forward to going in to work during the five years of my apprenticeship.

One of the aspects about working in the docks was the assumption by the ordinary public that those of us who did so, had access to all kinds of illicit goods. In some ways this was correct, although we might have had access within the docks, it was generally not worth the risk, especially where apprentices were concerned to attempt to take anything illegal through the gates. There was always a plentiful supply of tinned fruit, especially on ships returning from South Africa, so that when working on the boiler tops or in the crankcase of a main diesel engine a tin of peaches always went down well.

The dockers had their own way of broaching the cargo, I quite often noticed them signal to the crane driver to

The writer with his 1932 Rolls Royce 20/25 Park Ward Saloon, which he purchased in part exchange for his 1930 Phantom Two in 1960.

drop a pallet of whisky the last few feet, so that some of the bottles broke. As the precious liquid leaked out from underneath, the dockers would collect it in various containers and afterwards have an alcoholic tea break. One of their other dodges was to drill a small hole in the top of a barrel of rum just big enough to get a drinking straw into. When they were finished they would plug the hole with a small piece of wood, it was quite common to see a couple of straws sticking out of the top pocket of the waistcoat or jacket of the dockers who worked on the rum quays. I once saw the whole gang down in the hold of a Harrison line ship practically paralytic after broaching a cargo of neat rum. However these were not commonplace occurrences.

Chapter Twenty One

The Lascars

We were always being offered watches, cigarettes and lighters by the Lascar crews on the 'City Boats'. The watches were rubbish usually picked up in Suez or perhaps on the Continent, the Lascars took a great risk in trying to sell such items to the shore gangs, if they were discovered it would mean instant dismissal. We used to have some amusing moments with the Lascars, generally we got on quite well with them, but sometimes they could be very vindictive. On occasions we would arrange a little trick or two on them, sometimes we would let them think that we were interested in their wares of contraband. This was done by pretending to look closely at a selection lighters or watches, from the top of the engine room one of the heavy gang would be watching and when the time was right, he would put on a peaked hat just like the customs men wore and start to come down into the engine room. Someone then shouted, 'customs,' and the Lascars disappeared faster than cockroaches at the flick of a light switch. This then left us holding a couple of dozen watches or so, which were then quickly distributed among the lads. When things had calmed down and they thought the coast was clear they would return and say to the person that they thought they had left the goods with.

"You got watches Johnny."

To which the answer would be something like,

"No I don't want watch, see other men." This was said with a wave of the arm in the general direction of the rest of the workforce. Having become confused one of the Lascars would then approach someone else, only to be told the same thing. Working on the assumption that we all looked generally alike to them, as they did to us, we found that in the main the rouse usually worked.

Most of the Lascars were a jovial type of people with a sense of humour who took it with a good heart, on these occasions the goods were returned to them with smiles all round. There were some however that really turned nasty, calling us English pigs and spat at us, on these occasions we had to watch our backs, as they were not averse to dropping heavy spanners down on us from the top of the engine room. Luckily there was so much pipework above, we were able to hear them coming as they crashed and bounced their way down.

One of the things they always did, was to take the pieces of rag from the pockets of our boiler suits when we left them hanging on the hand rails at the top of the engine room overnight. This was because they were not issued with any rag from the ship's stores, the only cleaning materiel they were given was a rough coconut fibre which was pretty useless for cleaning purposes. One of the tricks we used to play on them was to place a nice lump of white rag on the engine room plates, to this we tied a length of thread which we led to a suitable hiding place. As soon as one of the Lascars spotted the rag he would slowly creep towards it, at the same time looking all round to make sure no one was watching; just as he was about to pick it up we would give the line a good pull, sending the rag off across the plates. This little trick never failed to terrify the unfortunate victim, who usually fled screaming for the nearest flight of steps. It was important to keep well hidden and not to laugh, so as to let them think there was some mysterious force at work.

It didn't take much to frighten them, I remember an occasion when we were working on the 'City of Lyons,' we were going to lunch and had reached the top of the engine room next to the stores, inside the stores was the 'Cassaub' [pronounced Kasab] or storekeeper. He was quite a small person, probably under five feet in height, as I reached the top grating I noticed he was sorting through some spare boiler valves at the back of the stores which was a compartment with no windows or grills at all, so that when the door was closed it became a sealed compartment. As we passed the stores, one of the engine room staff who happened to be a huge Sikh was just going in. Peter looked at me with his mischievous smile as his eyebrows rose above his horned rimmed glasses and he moved back against the handrail and indicated for me to squeeze by. As soon as I was clear he leaned over and shut the door to the stores and locked it using the key that was still in the lock, he also turned off the light from the switch which was outside the stores.

"That should be interesting, its about time we made ourselves scarce," he said, as he rubbed his hands together.

On our return from lunch, we found that quite a crowd had gathered around the engine room entrance, the people nearest were looking through and giving a running commentary to those on the fringes about something that was happening inside.

"What's going on," asked Dick.

Someone replied that the Cassaub had gone berserk and was killing somebody in the stores. They let us get by, so that we could climb down the first ladder to the grating outside the stores, this was also crowded with Lascars who were in a state of frenzy, in the middle of them was the second engineer, who was doing his best to calm them down. They were all too frightened to unlock the door to the stores, from inside we could hear someone screaming in a terrified manner, this was accompanied by a loud banging on the door with some kind of metal object.

Peter asked the second engineer why no one was unlocking the door. The second who was an Australian replied.

"Christ mate, do you want to get hacked to pieces, these fellows get real annoyed when you upset them."

Peter stepped forward, unlocked the door and pushed it open, as he did so the crowd on the grating made a hasty retreat either up to the engine room door or down below to the depths of the engine room. Peter on the other hand, had the advantage of knowing who was locked in the stores. The moment the door was opened, the huge Sikh came out with a look on his face that could only be described as sheer terror. The little Cassaub never bothered to come out, and as Dick switched on the light we were somewhat apprehensive as to what we would see inside. To our complete surprise and

174

amazement the little store keeper had a beaming smile that seemed to go from ear to ear, and was still sorting through the spares exactly as he had been doing when Peter had locked him in with the Sikh over an hour before. Later Peter explained that it was all to do with their religion and the different casts that had upset the huge Sikh, he said it had been too good an opportunity to miss even if it had got a bit out of hand.

On another occasion Big Arthur was making his way from the stokehole into the engine room, to do this you had to negotiate a narrow passage between the boilers, from the opposite direction came two Lascars about to go on watch in the boiler room, as they didn't move aside Arthur just barged between them, knocking them both over on their backs. He continued on into the engine room, but a short time later a large group of Lascars surrounded him in a threatening manor. Apparently this sort of behavior was customary in their own country when they had a grievance with their employer over pay or conditions, they would completely surround the person concerned and although they didn't resort to violence, their attitude was very threatening. Big Arthur was not prepared to let himself get caught in a situation that he couldn't get out of, so he laid into the ones nearest to him, knocking them out cold. The result was complete bedlam, Lascars appeared from everywhere, they were shouting abuse and throwing anything that came to hand at him. He had no alternative but to retreat backwards up the engine room ladders, fending them off as he did so. This continued all the way to the top of the gangway, where he was able to get clear of the ship, followed by a hail of missiles. To keep the peace the charge hand told the second engineer that he had given Arthur the sack, but he just transferred him to another ship the next day.

Chapter Twenty Two
Loyalty

During the last year of my time, we began to hear disturbing rumours about a pending apprentices strike in the shipyards in the North. This was very worrying, as by rights and according to our indentures we were not to take part in any industrial disputes. Things became quite serious as the strike moved further South. I never met an apprentice who wanted to go on strike, so I could only assume that it had been instigated by the unions with the excuse that they were trying to get more money in the wage packets of the apprentices, however I suspected there were ulterior motives as far as the unions were concerned. The Graving Docks apprentices were firmly against any strike action and decided that no matter what the outcome of the various meetings that followed, these were held in Canning Town, we were not going to come out on strike. To be effective, strike action would have to make a financial impact to the firms concerned, as in theory the apprentices were non-productive, I failed to see what difference it would make to the employers. The other more important aspect was that when we signed our indentures at the beginning of our five year term, we knew exactly what our minimum wage was going to be. In my first year it stated that I would receive £2. 17s. 6d [£2.87] per week, rising in increments to £5. 2s. 6d [£5. 27] in my fifth year.

What I didn't know before I started, was that with overtime, the P.B.R. bonus, and the special rates for working in certain areas of the ship, or with nasty substances such as crude oil, we ended up with much more, this was especially so once we went 'outside'. During the last year of my time I probably averaged around £20 or £30 a week, which in 1960 was a considerable sum.

By contrast, when I first went to sea as a Junior Engineer my salary was £47 per month, there was no paid overtime, we did get paid extra for Sundays at sea, and we also received what was known as a section 'A' bonus. However this did include food which was always excellent.

As I have mentioned before, apprenticeships in the London Docks were hard to get, having been lucky enough to have been accepted by the Graving Dock, I wasn't prepared to jeopardise my good fortune by entering into any strike action instigated by outsiders. Fortunately the strike never came to anything as far as the ship repair yards on the Thames were concerned, so we never had to stand and be counted.

Chapter Twenty Three
Final Voyage

The last few weeks of my five years seemed to fly by, for the last three, we found ourselves working on the 'Link Two,' which like the 'Link One,' the engine of which we had rebored down at Rochester three years previously were part of the recently formed Link Line belonging to the Coast Lines Group. The Graving Dock carried out a considerable amount of work on the 'Link Two' while she was berthed alongside their quay in Blackwall Basin. She took up the whole length of the quay plus a good bit more. Her bows came halfway across the caisson of the dry dock and her stern reached the far side of the entrance to Junction Dock.

Like the Link One, she was powered by a triple expansion steam engine, our job was to strip and check all the bearings including the crossheads and guides, we then had to rebuild it with all the correct clearances. The engine room was full of fitters, boilermakers, heavy gang, welders and their mates, plus the various apprentices. As most of the men wore heavy boots with steel toe caps and studded soles, in such a crowded area, the welders would be in their element. If you were standing on a grating and a welder was working underneath, extra vigilance was required because they were inclined to weld your boots to the grating by the studs on the soles.

As the job neared completion, we were told that we would be going on trials with her, just in case there were any problems. The day before the sea trials the ship's engineers flashed up the boilers and checked that all the valves were working. Once they were satisfied, the main engine was started and run for a few minutes, then stopped while we felt all the bearings to make sure they were not getting warm. When everything had been checked the engine was restarted and run for fifteen minutes, after which it was again stopped and everything rechecked. This procedure was followed, doubling up the running time until it was kept running for an hour, after which the chief engineer said he was satisfied with the way everything was running and was happy to take the ship to sea.

The next morning we joined the ship at 7 o'clock, the Graving Dock crew consisted of Peter, Dick, and myself, plus another fitter and his mate and Jake their apprentice. There were also four heavy gang and two boilermakers with their mates, the charge hand and his runner also came along, making sixteen in all. The arrangements were, that provided everything went well, the ship would heave to about three miles off Southend and we would then transfer to a tug and be taken to the end of Southend pier. There would be a lorry and a mini-bus waiting at the shore end of the pier to take us back to the yard.

While the crew made ready for sea, we made ourselves scarce in the mess room with copious amounts of tea. There were two small tugs standing by to assist the ship out of Blackwall Basin into the Import Dock and then through to the South Dock, where she entered the locks ready for her trip down the Thames. Just after 9am we entered the river and the second engineer who was at the controls slowly increased the rev's up to her normal sea speed of 102 rpm. During the voyage down river we made regular visits to the engine room where we found everything running well, the second engineer giving us the thumbs up as we reached the control platform. For me to see a large triple expansion engine running at full speed was quite an experience. Although I had worked on dozens of these engines over the previous three years it was the first time I had seen one running at full speed under sea going conditions. The only way of describing an engine of this type running, especially at slow speed, is poetry in motion.

The voyage down river proved uneventful, and being the first week of July we were lucky to have the benefit of a fine sunny morning, so we were able to stretch out on the forward cargo hatch and enjoy the view. There was plenty to see, with ships moored at the various wharves discharging their cargo's from all parts of the world, as we came into Gallions Reach one of New Zealand Shipping Company's

179

vessels the 8213 ton gross, 'Rakaia' which was built in 1945 was just entering the locks to the Royal Albert Dock on the final stage of her six week voyage from the Antipodes. This was one of her first trips since having her main engine rebuilt by her makers Harland and Wolff following a serious engine failure in 1957 about 700 miles out of New York bound for Manchester. One of her piston rods broke, causing extensive damage to the main engine and one of the generators. The engineers toiled night and day to effect repairs while the ship drifted in heavy seas to the Latitude of Bermuda. Eventually after stripping out all the damaged parts and rigging up makeshift bypass systems they managed to get the engine running on six out of her eight cylinders.

While the engineers worked non stop down below, the deck crew who were nearly all cadets rigged up steadying sails from hatch covers. The combind efforts of all the crew enabled the 'Rakaia' to eventually reach Liverpool with her valuable cargo of frozen meat. I did not know it then, but I was later to serve aboard her for two voyages as her third engineer, although she was hard work, she proved to be a happy ship.

Shortly after leaving the 'Rakaia' astern we rounded Barking Reach and passed Dagenham Dock, then Phoenix Wharf at Rainham and on passed Bowater's jetty on the South bank at Northfleet where I had so often worked. Laying off in mid-stream was the Sarah Bowater and tied up stern to, at the jetty was the Constance Bowater, their dark green hulls and creamy white topsides standing out in the morning sun. I could see that the Constance Bowater had nearly completed the discharge of her cargo of newsprint from Canada, as she was riding high in the water.

The river was a myriad of shipping and it was difficult to decide where to look next, there seemed to be craft of all types going in all directions. I recognised the Ocean Coast owned by Coast Lines, she was 1173 tons and built in 1935. We had done a considerable amount of work on her in the dry dock at the Graving Dock about two years previously. She was making the most of the ebb tide to get clear of the estuary to begin her voyage.

As Tilbury landing stage came into view, I could see a large white P&O liner laying alongside, as we drew closer I could see it was the 'Chusan' she was 24062 tons gross, and built in 1950. By a strange coincidence my cousin Peter Base was Chief Refrigeration Officer aboard her, he had served his apprenticeship with J&E Halls at Dartford, and had been at sea for many years. Just after passing Tilbury we felt the rev's drop, and thinking the worst, made a dash for the engine room, where we found the second engineer calmly leaning on the engine room desk drinking coffee from a huge enamel mug. He gave us the thumbs up and indicated that they had slowed down to let the river pilot off. We were soon under way again and it wasn't long before we had Southend Pier on our Port beam, as we drew level with the pier I heard the telegraph ring and felt the engine slow down, looking ahead I could see a large tug coming towards us. Peter, Dick and myself went below to carry out a final check on the bearings.

The third engineer moved the telegraph lever in response

The New Zealand Shipping Company's 8563 ton gross M.V. 'Rakaia'. Launched in 1945 as the Empire Abercorn. The author did his first trip to sea aboard her as a junior engineer and later did two voyages as her 3rd engineer.
Seen here outward bound with a general cargo to Pitcairn Island, Fiji, Samoa and New Zealand from London's Royal Albert Dock via the Panama Canal.
Photographed by Foto Flite, Ashford, Kent.

to 'stop engine' and the second engineer brought the engine to a stop. Before we checked the bearings we called the bridge to let them know we were going to do so, and that the ship would be without engines for the next ten minutes. Peter insisted, that the turning gear was engaged before we climbed around the engine feeling all the bearings to make sure they were not running hot.

Having satisfied ourselves that all was well, we said our farewells to the ships engineer's and joined the rest of the men who had already boarded the tug which was now alongside. The heavy gang had also transferred all the chain blocks and tool boxes, so we were soon under way heading towards the pier head, about three miles away. The Link Two gave us a long blast on her steam whistle, and with plenty of black smoke pouring from her funnel, indicating that the donkeyman wasn't giving the boiler enough draught, she soon disappeared into the heat haze.

When we arrived at the end of the pier we had to get all the equipment up to the top, it was fortunate that the sea was calm and it was slack water, otherwise it would have been a tricky operation, especially with a heavy sea running. Arrangements had been made, so that everything could be

Coast Lines 1173 tons gross Ocean Coast (1935) seen underway after being dry docked at The London Graving Dock for extentisve repairs, following collision damage to her stern quarter.
(Duncan Mackenzie)

loaded on to the small train that ran along the pier, once all the gear was on board we jumped on for the two mile ride to the shore end of the pier. On arrival we set up a chain and passed everything along to the pavement where it was piled up to await the arrival of the lorry.

We hung around for a few minutes, but as there was no sign of our transport and the pub on the opposite side of the road was looking more inviting by the second, it was unanimously decided that we would leave everything on the pavement and go across the road for a quick beer, where we would also be able to keep an eye out for the arrival of the lorry and minibus. It wasn't long before the table tops were stacked with pint glasses, being a hot day we all downed several pints in quick succession and seriously depleted the establishments stock of meat pies. Someone said that the lorry had arrived, so the heavy gang went over and soon had all the gear loaded ready for the trip back to the yard. Being July it was the height of the summer season, the pub was crowded with day trippers mostly from the London area, so by the time the drivers joined us there was a good old knees up going on. As is often the case in situations like this, everyone forgot about the time, until the landlord shouted last orders for the afternoon, by which time most of us didn't know what day of the week it was.

The two drivers were legless and quite incapable of driving, so it looked like we were going to be stuck in Southend for some considerable time. As luck would have it one of the heavy gang was big Joe Dunn, Joe had the constitution of a large sponge and was able to absorb vast quantities of ale without any visible effects, it was therefore left to him to get the lorry back to the yard. The minibus was another matter, but again we were in luck as one of the boiler makers said that his mate was practically a teetotaller, and had been drinking shandy for most of the time. Once the charge hand had satisfied himself that the boilermakers mate was in a fit state to drive, it was obvious that the chargehand was in the same condition as the mini-bus driver and quite incapable of making that sort of judgement, never the less the boilermakers mate was deemed fit enough to drive, more by necessity than prudence, we all piled in and set off for the journey back to the Isle of Dogs.

We eventually arrived back at about 6pm I had left the Rolls parked round the back of the fitters shop, but Peter said it would be advisable if we slept it off for a while, as we were still in no fit state to drive home, especially in the rush hour through Blackwall Tunnel. It was still very hot so we clambered up on to the giant Greenheart logs that were stacked at the back of the fitting shop and immediately fell asleep.

The next thing I remember was being woken by Peter, when I came to my senses I realised that it was almost dark, so it must have been about 9:30pm.

"Feeling fit," inquired Peter.

"Except for a thick head and a chronic backache, not too bad," I replied.

"Well we had better be on our way, I'll follow you through as far as Charlton," he replied.

The place was deserted except for us, so what had become of the rest of the lads remained a mystery, as I seem to remember one or two of them were in a bit of a bad way. I somehow arrived home safely, had the dinner my mother kept warm for me and went to bed. The next morning I set off to work with mixed feelings, on the one hand I was quite upset that this was going to be my last day at the Graving Dock, yet on the other, it meant a whole new chapter of my life was about to begin. I still hadn't made up my mind which shipping company I would like to join, it was becoming a difficult decision to make, as in terms of choice the world was my oyster.

There was a shortage of qualified applicants for sea going positions, so most of the companies were offering very good terms to attract first trippers.

My last day was spent saying goodbye to all the friends that I had made during the last five years. Unfortunately, some like Sid were working on ships out of the area such as the Royal Albert Dock, and I found myself wishing that I was down there as well, perhaps pulling out a couple of bottom ends in readiness for the surveyor the following day, and looking forward to a nice bit of overtime.

The events of the previous days outing to Southend were the main subject of conversation when I joined Peter and Dick in the stores, from what I could tell, everyone who went on the sea trial managed to get home safely, and all turned up for work that morning. We went over to The Gun at lunch time, but kept it within reason, mainly because we were still feeling some what delicate from the day before. Little did I realise that it would be my last pint there for the next thirty five years, when my companions would then be my wife and grandchildren. Although there were only two other customers in the bar at the time, I had the strange feeling that many more were present.

During the afternoon all my old colleagues in the fitting shop presented me with a camera. This took me by surprise and left me speechless, they said it would do to record all my future voyages with, as it happens I still have it and consider it one of my most prized possessions.

Towards the end of the day I went across to the main office to collect my indentures, a very important document that proved I had completed my five years training and education towards being a marine engineer. One of the girls in the office, who happened to be Dick's niece, showed me into Edgar Taylor's office with a look that told me that Edgar was in one of his usual bad moods.

Being as I still had an hour or so to go before my apprenticeship was complete, I knew that I still had to be careful how I handled the interview.

As I entered his office I was greeted with,

"Who the bloody hell are you, and what's more what do you want."

He knew full well who I was, but as usual he was trying to make things as unpleasant as possible. I told him my name and that I had come for my indentures.

"I haven't got time to mess about with things like that, you'll have to come back another day," he ranted as he ushered me out of his office, adding as he did so,

"See that girl, what's her name, that showed you in, get her to sort it out."

Indenture

This Indenture made the **Ninth** day of **July,** One Thousand Nine Hundred and **Fifty-six** WITNESSETH THAT **David John Carpenter,** of **39, Highmead, Plumstead, S.E.18,** (hereinafter called the Apprentice) in the County of **London,** Son or Ward of **Henry Edward Carpenter** (hereinafter called the Guardian) by and with the consent and approbation of **Henry Edward Carpenter** testified by **Himself** executing these presents doth put himself Apprentice to **The London Graving Dock Company Limited** of whose Registered Office is situate at **Prestons Road, Poplar, E.14.** (hereinafter called the Master) to learn the Art, Trade or Business of **Engineer.** and to serve them as an Apprentice from the **Ninth** day of **July, 1956** for a term of **Five** years thence next ensuing subject to the provisions hereinafter contained.

The Apprentice and Guardian hereby bind themselves jointly and severally that he, the Apprentice, shall faithfully serve, obey and comply with all lawful regulations and instructions issued by the Master and shall not absent himself without permission from the Master's services but in all things as a faithful Apprentice shall behave himself towards the Master during the said term.

And that he, the Apprentice, will make up all lost time at the end of each year of the said term before a further year of service hereunder is deemed to commence, and for the purpose of this clause time shall be deemed lost in any of the following cases, namely :

(a) Abstention from service under these presents on account of sickness or other physical incapacity unless a Doctor's Certificate is produced or sent by post addressed to the Manager of the Works of the Master, at which the apprentice is serving, within three days of the commencement of such absence. Provided always that if such absence medically certified as aforesaid shall exceed in any one year of the said term, a period of four weeks, all absence or absences from the services of the Master in excess of such period of four weeks shall be deemed to be lost time.

(b) Abstention from service under these presents from any other cause whatsoever unless leave of absence is previously granted by the Master's Manager of the Works at which the Apprentice is serving at the time.

And that he, the Apprentice, shall be punctual in his attendance at the Works and also shall work such number of works hours of each working day as may be reasonably directed by the Master, and shall attend regularly and work diligently at such further educational classes at least twice a week, for instruction in technical matters at such times and places as the Master may indicate to the Apprentice.

The Master reserves the right to dismiss the Apprentice and to annul and cancel this indenture for any breach thereof or of the lawful rules and regulations affecting an Apprentice of the Master for the time being or for misbehaviour, disobedience or unfaithfulness on the part of the Apprentice towards the Master, or in the event of the Apprentice losing time in the manner hereinbefore defined for any period or periods together exceeding three calendar months during any year of the said term. Such cancellation of the indenture by the Master as aforesaid shall be effected by notices in writing, delivered or sent by registered post to the Guardian and to the Apprentice at their usual or last known place or places of address and signed for and on behalf of the Master by the Secretary or any authorised person for the time being.

The Apprentice shall not authorise or knowingly consent to any Trade Union or any official or agent or member thereof interfering in any matter between him and the Master.

The Apprentice shall not take part in any way whatsoever in any labour dispute the Master may have with any of his employees or in which the Master or any of his employees may be involved, and shall during the continuance of any such labour dispute, do all such work as he may be lawfully required to perform, and as the Master shall direct to be done.

The Master will not be responsible for any interruption or stoppage of the term of service hereinbefore mentioned due to strikes, lockouts, labour troubles or other causes beyond his control.

Subject, as aforesaid, the Master shall in consideration of the services of the Apprentice, teach and instruct the Apprentice in the said trade or business by the best means in his power, and shall pay the Apprentice the following wages which shall, however, be subject to variation up or down in accordance with national fluctuations of apprentices' time rates.

	During the 1st year at the rate of				per week	
„	„ 2nd „	„	„	„		„
„	„ 3rd „	„	„	„		„
„	„ 4th „	„	„	„		„
„	„ 5th „	„	„	„		„

If during any week of the said term, time shall have been lost, a proportionate deduction from the weekly wages payable to the Apprentice shall be made in respect of such lost time.

Upon completion of the said term these presents shall be handed over to the Apprentice with a certificate of service endorsed thereon and signed by or on behalf of the Master, constituting a testimonial such as in the opinion of the Master shall have been merited by the Apprentice. And for the true performance of all and every of the said Covenants and Agreements, the said parties bind themselves.

In Witness whereof the said parties have hereunto set their hands and seals the day and year first above written.

Signed, Sealed and Delivered by the Apprentice in the presence of:
Edward N/Askew

David J. Carpenter.

Signed, Sealed and Delivered by the Guardian in the presence of:

H. E. Carpenter.

Signed, Sealed and Delivered for and on behalf of the Master, by a Director, Manager or Secretary in the presence of:

For and on behalf of
THE LONDON GRAVING DOCK CO. LIMITED
SECRETARY.

I went back down the corridor to see Dick's niece, and as I reached her desk she handed me a large brown envelope and said.

"The grumpy old bastard can't help it, most of its put on really, he got me to prepare your indentures at the beginning of the week, so I had better give them to you now, just in case he goes into one of his rages and tears them up, good luck Dave."

I thanked her, and as I walked back across the overhead corridor that spanned the yard entrance, Edgar opened his door and shouted.

"At least I won't have to put up with that bloody Rolls-Royce coming in the yard anymore," then slammed the door shut.

It so happened that I had left the Rolls at home that morning, just in case things had got out of hand over at The Gun, so it was with a heavy heart that I boarded the bus for the trip round the Island to the foot tunnel at Island Gardens for the last time.

In hindsight the five years of my apprenticeship were probably the best years of my life. Not only had I learnt all the basic skills that would stand me in good stead for the rest of my working life as a marine engineer, I had also unconsciously learnt how to get on with my fellow workers, and respect other peoples points of view. In particular this ability helped make my future sea going years a very pleasurable experience.

It is a pity that today's youngsters have been denied the opportunity of serving a proper five year apprenticeship in their chosen profession, as I feel that to be able to work on even terms with experienced people who are keen to pass on their skills, can only be good for the country as a whole, mainly in improving the social attitude and the moral respect of their fellow human beings.

This was my reason for giving this account of life in the London Docks as seen through the eyes of 16 to 21 year old, the title of Dockland Apprentice. Not only did I learn all the practical skills while at the London Graving Dock, my apprenticeship greatly benefited me in the transition from schoolboy to manhood and on throughout the rest of my working life.

Addendum

I continued my association with the London Docks for several years after the completion of my apprenticeship. This was in the capacity as an engineer with the New Zealand Shipping Company. Their home port was Londons Royal Albert Dock and their berths were up at the North West end, by the cold storage warehouses, the next berth up was the banana berth where I had often worked on ships such as the 'Jamaica Producer'. This meant that many of my voyages began and ended from The Royal Albert Dock.

The Docks were still very busy during this period i.e. 1960 – 68, with no obvious sign of the forth coming drastic decline that was over the horizon. The demand for berths was so great that inward bound ships usually had to drop anchor off Southend, and sometimes had to wait for anything up to a week for a berth in The Docks.

During the 1970s, while I was working as works manager for a marine engineering firm on the South Coast, I had occasion to visit The King George V Dock to appraise and estimate the installation of new main engines on a small short sea trader. I crossed the river on the Woolwich Ferry, which since 1964 had seen the service replaced by three new diesel powered vessels; the old paddle steamers having been retired.

While crossing the river I suddenly realised that a great change had taken place, the ferry had lost those appealing qualities that had attracted me all those years before, there was no inviting smell wafting from the engine room and worse still, no access to it. Gone were the tall stove like funnels billowing clouds of black smoke, gone were the mysterious black signalling balls that hung from the forward funnel stay. Even the river had lost its unique pungent smell.

With a feeling of apprehension I noticed that there were no ships funnels towering above the houses and dominating the skyline on the North side. I arrived at the Eastern entrance to the Royal Group of docks in Woolwich Manor

Way, which was where I had first entered the docks thirty years before and could'nt believe my eyes. The whole dock seemed empty, gone were all those magnificent leviathans that had lured me to go to sea on my first visit. I pulled over to let the policeman on duty know who I was, and asked him where the ship was laying.

"You'll find her right up at the far end of the K.G. you can't miss her she's the only ship in there," he replied.

I told him that I used to work in the docks and how shocked I was at seeing all the desolation.

"Its all finished mate, I'am only hear today because there's a Clan boat discharging in the Albert, you'll see her as you go by. Be careful when you drive past, believe it or not the few docker's that are working her are having a dispute over working conditions and have all walked off the ship," he added in reply.

He waved me on, and as I came up towards the derelict looking Central Hotel I noticed a dozen or so docker's grouped around a central figure who was gesticulating with his arms in the air.

"Some things are still the same," I thought to myself.

I drove up the dock, passing the spot where Alf Hinds had converted his Riley after driving under the railway goods wagon in the smog all those years before, then the N.Z.S. Co berths, where their great ships, such as the 'Rangitane' and the 'Rangitoto' had discharged their cargo's and many a young man such as myself had joined his first ship at the start of an adventurous career at sea. Passing round the dry docks at the Eastern end of the docks I came to the top end of the King George V Dock, everywhere I looked were signs of neglect, there was not a person to be seen. All the sheds and buildings were still standing, but doors were either hanging off or missing altogether, windows were smashed and piles of litter were heaped up in the corners against walls, rubbish was strewn across the road and all the railway lines were red with rust.

I spotted my destination laying at the end of the dock, looking lost and forlorn in that vast empty expanse of water stretching over half a mile back to the entrance lock. The ship was called 'Polythene' a rusty old vessel of less than 1000 tons, she had the appearance of an Ex. Admiralty vessel and was powered by two Crossley Type HRL diesel engines.

As I got out of the car I was struck by the intense silence, except for a light wind that gently lifted a sheet of waste paper, there was no movement anywhere. I felt like the last person left at a holiday resort at the end of a Summer season. The re engining of the 'Polythene' was never carried, not because of our costing, but through the still powerful influence of the union. Through necessity the remaining ship repair firms on the river had been forced to amalgamate into one concern called 'River Thames Ship Repairers Ltd.' They were still strictly controlled by the unions, who under no circumstances would allow an outside non union firm to carry out work in the docks. We did consider bringing the 'Polythene' round to our yard on the South coast, but for various reasons thought better of it. That was the last encounter that I had with the union, but I watched while they led like Lemmings, their unenthusiastic members to a slow and eventual demise.

We were lucky on the South coast, we were able to continue in business for several more years repairing all types of ships including Ex Royal Mail Lines, 'Deseado' and 'Durango' and at the time under the Shaw Savill flag.

I also renewed my association with the London Graving Dock Company by sending several machining jobs up to them by lorry that were too big for the machine tools that we had in our workshop to handle. These were usually tailshafts that we had stripped out of vessels on the gridiron at Newhaven.

During this time I liaised with Edgar Hurd the company's secretary, whom I had known since my apprenticeship days.

There was also an occasion when he telephoned me to see if we would work all night to fit four new cargo fans to one of Ellermans 'City Boats,' this was to complete a job that had been started at Graving Dock in London. For reasons I can't recall, the ship had to sail from London before the job was finished and as she was making a brief stop at Newhaven he asked me if I could help.

The fans were delivered the afternoon before the ship was due, they arrived on the back of one of the Graving Docks familiar dark blue lorries, they were about six feet in diameter and came complete with sheets of jointing and all the nuts, bolts and washers to finish the job. With the fans came Don Anderson who was one of the under managers at the Graving Dock, I hadn't seen him since my apprenticeship days some fifteen years previously. He had no idea that I had worked at the Graving Dock until I mentioned this to him, he was unable to recall me as many apprentices had passed through The London Graving Dock Co. since my time.

However when I told him that I used to come to work in a Rolls Royce he roared with laughter saying he remembered the car well, mainly because Edgar Tayor the General Manager used to rant and rave about that bloody apprentice who owned a Rolls Royce, and every time he saw the car in the yard, he would storm into the office and make the girls get out all the time sheets.

We had a good laugh about old times and Don left us to return London, while we got on with the job, we finished at 8:30 the next morning and the ship sailed at midday.

I continued in the ship repair business, until the big ships became ugly and too big to use our facilities, and proper ships with graceful lines together with small coasters disappeared from our waters completely.

Gone are the docks that made young mens'
 dreams come true.
Lost are the skills that gave them their chance.
Grown old now those lucky young men and all the
 girls that they once new,
Gone are the ships that were full of romance.

Glossary

Caisson   A water tight barrier to a dry-dock that can be opened and shut. Sometimes has a road across the top of it.

Donkeyman   A person in charge of ships boilers and sometimes the engine room stores.

Dunnage   Lengths of timber, used to secure cargo down in the holds of ships.

Fidley   Series of ladders and gratings at the top of the boiler room that lead out to the base of the funnel.

Fo'castle   Forepart of a ship.

Gridiron   A series of parallel timbers, usually Greenheart, that enable a vessel to float on at high water. When the tide recedes the ship would be left high and dry, so that maintenance can be carried out to the underwater section of the hull.

Gunnel Fly   Nautical term 'fly on the wall'.

Indentured   Bound by contract to a master for a fixed term.

Lascar   Native crew member, usually recruited from India, or the Laccadive Islands.

mah-jongg   Chinese table game, played at great speed with ivory tiles.

Serang   Head native crew member.

Sill   Bottom of entrance to dry-dock.

Further reading on The London Graving Dock Company.

Eighty years of The London Graving Dock Company by Edgar Hurd.

A copy of this informative book can be read at The Museum in Docklands West India Dock Quay, Hertsmere Road London.

Contributions to the Maritime History of Great Britain by John Crighton.

A copy of this rare publication can be read at Tower Hamlets Museum where it was kindly donated by Mary Mills.